SUSTAINING HEART IN THE HEARTLAND

SUSTAINING HEART IN THE HEARTLAND

Exploring Rural Spirituality

Edited by
Miriam Brown, OP

The Rural Spirituality Team

Miriam Brown, OP, Rev. Dr. Barbara A. Pursey,
Rev. Karl Goodfellow, Rev. Diane Jochum,
Ambrose Koopmann, and Larry Tranel

Paulist Press
New York/Mahwah, N.J.

Cover design by Trudi Gershenov
Book design by Lynn Else

Library of Congress Cataloging-in-Publication Data

Sustaining heart in the heartland : exploring rural spirituality / edited by Miriam Brown.
p. cm.
Includes bibliographical references.
ISBN 0-8091-4319-4 (alk. paper)
1. Country life—Religious aspects—Christianity. 2. Rural churches—United States. I. Brown, Miriam.

BV638.S87 2005
277.3'083'091734—dc22

2004030502

Published by Paulist Press
997 Macarthur Boulevard
Mahwah, New Jersey 07430

www.paulistpress.com

Printed and bound in the
United States of America

CONTENTS

PREFACE

The Churches' Center for Land and People (CCLP), headquartered at Sinsinawa, Wisconsin, and cosponsored ecumenically, formed a rural spirituality dialogue group, headed by Miriam Brown, OP (Sinsinawa Dominican) and Rev. Dr. Barbara Pursey, (University of Dubuque Theological Seminary faculty, retired). Pastoral leaders, clergy and lay; farmers; those in agriculture-related occupations, institutions, and organizations; and others concerned for the spiritual vitality of rural communities gathered bimonthly to consider how spiritual formation/growth is manifest and can be nourished in the rural Midwest in its churches and communities.

Members of this group listened carefully to people's interactions in a variety of settings: homes and churches, field days and farm expos, congregation-sponsored faith-and-farm days, denominational conferences both national and local, university forums, social-service and parish nurse trainings, events and meetings of grassroots organizations, and annual conferences of CCLP and the Center for Theology and Land (CTL) of Wartburg and University of Dubuque Seminaries in Dubuque, Iowa. They listened for the Spirit and pursued descriptions and concerns. Who are the people and groups who make up rural communities and what are the special features and contributions of their spiritual lives? What has formed and what now fosters their spiritual development and growth? How is spirituality lived out in individual and communal decisions and actions? What today may erode or obstruct healthy and sustaining spirituality? How can clergy and laity work together to foster and nurture the spiritual vigor of the rural community?

A generous writing team of six emerged to shape what was learned. *Sustaining Heart in the Heartland* articulates insights and suggests pastoral ways of growing, working, and ministering in the rural community. Dedication over many years has produced this book as a gift to the rural community. It is offered with love.

Miriam Brown, OP, Churches' Center for Land and People, initiating executive director. *Cochair, writer, editor.*

Rev. Dr. Barbara A. Pursey, University of Dubuque Theological Seminary, retired. *Cochair, writer.*

Rev. Karl Goodfellow, rural pastor, Safety Net Prayer Ministry. *Writer.*

Rev. Diane Jochum, rural pastor, spiritual guidance ministry. *Writer.*

Ambrose Koopmann, third-generation family farmer, lay minister. *Writer.*

Larry Tranel, Iowa State University Extension, Agriculture. *Writer.*

Sustaining Heart in the Heartland was written so that people of the heartland in all their variety and richness would find themselves in it, rejoice in their call, and consciously nurture their gifts of faith and hope and love, their deep spirituality. It was written for those in ministry, clergy and lay leaders, to understand rural spirituality in and beyond traditional borders of congregational life, toward the fostering of the life of grace in the whole community's interconnected life.

The authors wrote it with passion for rural life, and an ever-growing appreciation for rural spirituality that they found to be—whether expressed by the churched or unchurched—deeply rooted, communal, and contributing. The book celebrates the reality of rural life's special land-God connection and the vocation of stewardship. It illustrates that rural spirit and spirituality involve dependence on and commitment to complex and demanding interrelationships, with responsibility to the "common good" lived out close-up every day.

Rural spirituality is tough and generous. It is important to the world that in the heartland people are working together on their part of the planet's critical questions of today. How do we love our neighbor? How do we care for the earth? How do we "do" interdependence, sustainability, dignity, and justice in a changing and interconnected world?

By making the spirit of rural spirituality more conscious in rural culture, in church life, and beyond, not only can its vulnerabilities be better cared for, but its strengths can be offered to a world in need.

ACKNOWLEDGMENTS

Our acknowledgments begin with honoring heartland people who are the inspiration of this book. Rural and small-town people are large of soul, caring for the earth and each other. May they find our deep respect in everything we wrote. They enrich our country every day with their knowledge and personal dedication that is caring, prophetic, steadfast, and visionary. We are grateful to be part of this generous heart.

We thank the congregations and committed rural ministers of the heartland who with generous faith give their love and ministry to the community. They have given us insight into the concerns and spirituality of the people. May they themselves be sustained in spirit.

We thank the generous members of grassroots organizations and institutions who gift rural life with energy and vision, naming the issues and doing the hard work of educating and organizing for stewardship and justice. Their networks are places of hope and their gatherings energized by courage and the Spirit.

We thank the board members of the Churches' Center for Land and People for their ongoing seriousness about mission and their encouragement of this book. We honor the thirty church judicatories and religious orders of Wisconsin, Iowa, and Illinois who during the time of our writing have given witness to their commitment to rural life and ministry as Sponsors and Patrons of the Churches' Center for Land and People.

We thank the many people gloriously filling our book—people from farms, communities, and networks. They gift the land and people with their commitment every day. Special thanks to all who have enriched our annual CCLP Rural Life Gatherings at Sinsinawa, facilitating the lively exchanges and rituals. We honor especially the members of CCLP's committees: Earth Stewardship, Renewal, Ethics, and Rural Spirituality who shared year after year what the rural heart is all about.

Thank you to Jane McGrain, OSF, who typed and retyped as we shaped the text over the years. We thank Patricia A. Lynch of Harvest Graphics whose early offer to prepare the book for self- publishing encouraged us to move ahead. We are grateful to Rev. Lawrence Boadt, CSP, President of Paulist Press, who accepted our first draft, and to Paul McMahon, Managing Editor, who moved the final edition into production. Both weathered our breathless urgency to get it into print.

Finally, we of the writing committee need to thank each other for the firm commitment that kept us together from our diverse worlds over many years of exploration, shaping, and writing. A more faithful and encouraging group could not have been found.

Thank you, ever loving God. You sustain our hearts and hold us together in your love. Bless all of us in this heart-land of your care. Amen

INTRODUCTION: GEOGRAPHY OF FAITH

This is holy ground, we're standing on holy ground,
For the Lord is present and where God is is holy.
(From the hymn "Holy Ground,"
by Christopher Beatty)

Many a heartland gathering has begun with this holy reminder ringing in our ears and touching our hearts. As a Dominican sister on mission, I have experienced a variety of "holy grounds": university towns, inner city, Appalachia, the Midwest. With each move I have immersed myself in the workings, concerns, meanings, and relationships of those distinct geographies where God's tent has been pitched and where the people's faith is special to the place. Where we *are* is where God celebrates and mourns, thunders against what is death-dealing, and holds in tender hands communities of life. It is wonderful to belong to the community of church that celebrates this—and to be that church, alive, responsive, and struggling in the geography of faith given to us.

When I was in the "coalfields" of West Virginia in the mid-1980s, a member of the Committee on Religion in Appalachia observed, "We are poor, but we have something to teach from our experience. The Midwest is next." The words stuck in my heart because he was talking about my heartland home. Just as the people of the Appalachian Mountains had long ago lost their land and livelihoods to "big coal," he was saying, so would the fields of the rural heartland suffer the inroads of corporate control. When I returned to the Midwest in 1989, farmers, churches, and organizations were worn out from the "farm crisis of the eighties." At the invitation of the Sinsinawa Dominican Sisters, forty-two representatives of church bodies and grassroots organizations gathered to describe what it felt like "out there": debt, grief, isolation; fragmented efforts of churches and organizations; spiritual exhaustion. They wanted to work together. Over the fifteen years of the Churches' Center for Land and People (CCLP), the crisis has turned chronic. Merger after merger has tied the food system into a few major corporations and robbed farmers not only of their local networks, fair prices, and qualitative living, but of their heartfelt sense of vocation.

But that is not the whole story. The meanings of CCLP's Call Statement and then our Mission Statement have grown in us with the years. "This we share..." has revealed the rich and vibrant quilt of interrelationships. We have worked in rural ways to "strengthen bonds;" to "integrate earth stewardship, community, spirituality, and justice;" and to act as "a voice within our churches and society." Grace, we found, abounds.

This is holy ground. The geography of the heartland rolls and bends with the rivers, spreads out in vast fields of grains and grasses, is windswept and sunlit under an expanding, ever-changing sky. It is marked off in farmsteads and towns, criss-crossed with roads of connection and commerce, with county buildings, churches, expo centers, and grain bins marking the places of gathering. Rural people commit themselves to place for generations. We are rooted people—rooted in soil, rejoicing in the partnership of farmers, rain, and earthworms, and the intricate workings of the nature we are part of.

How, we ask, to be church, *here*?—to experience in the land the God of earth and spirit; to be a people of close-knit family and community; to share the load of long hours and worry-filled seasons; to face controlled markets and the threat of technological and corporate powers; to nurture community through family reunions, church worship, county fairs, and town festivals.

Every year after harvest and through the winter rural people travel country roads to community-like gatherings for annual meetings, church conferences, strategizing sessions, and network-building. At the Churches' Center for Land and People, a kind of microcosm of the whole, we come together from four states to give thanks, to complain (a right and proper biblical thing to do), to strengthen our commitments, and to be renewed. We are stretched into each other's lives and issues, connecting in care and solidarity, believing in the God present and the challenge ahead. We share stories of witness about earth stewardship, pastoral care, and political action from our widening circles. We are a rural-life quilt of farmers, clergy and lay leaders, urban connections, educators, service professionals, organizers, and advocates. The lines blur between teaching and learning, church and public life, clergy and lay, theorists, practitioners, and activists. We are the place for heart and call.

I love this book, rising from the heartland experience and shepherded by the Rural Spirituality writing team. The book mirrors back to people their *strengths* so that the social and economic challenges do not overwhelm. I hope the active faith-full people reading this will feel the power of their "call" in their daily places of action, and be encouraged in recognizing each group's contribution to the whole. We want everyone to realize that *they* are the sustainers of heart in the heartland. Together we participate in an evolving vision for this holy ground. As rural people we claim the wealth of our heritage and regroup for a new and renewed agricultural community. The stories and actions of the people described here link our heartland vocations to those larger currents of today's global call: interdependence, sustainability, community, dignity, and justice.

What is asked of us in this time and place? What great traditions of faith and hope, what deep habits of stewardship and communal generosity can we draw upon? As churches and people of spirit, we must work together and pray: resist unjust concentration of power, protect the relationships of community and the earth-wisdom of family farms, and create alternative systems for the health of the land and people now and into the future. This is our spiritual task. We give our souls to it. *Sustaining Heart in the Heartland* is our celebration and call. This is holy ground and where we are is holy.

Miriam Brown, OP

PART ONE

Rural Spirituality

The four chapters of Part One spread out before the reader several patterns of the quilt of rural spirituality—its characteristics and themes, its glory and its hurt.

Spirituality has to do with that pull of God deep within us—of desire, hope, and summons. It sets afire our longings to be generous, to be good, to have purpose, to care. It stirs our energies for love, work, and concern beyond ourselves. It challenges us in our pain and our dreams, our failures, and our ache for a deep relationship.

Rural spirituality, as we begin to describe it in Part One and exemplify it in Part Two, has everything to do with that deep-seated hope and desire that rises from the land into our souls. This call of God is exacting of our faithfulness and challenges the hope of our faltering hearts. It gathers us as a people of the heartland. "Whom shall I send?" asks our God in our presence. We answer, over and over again, "Send us!"

CHAPTER 1

INTERCONNECTEDNESS OF THE RURAL HEART

We assume you bring to this study, or will learn from it, a love for rural life: the land, the people, the spirit. Read to find yourself in it as participants and ministers, and to understand the rich complexity of the living patchwork quilt of graced relationships. This is a hard time in rural America, a necessary time to reflect together on the rural heritage of strength, faith, and community in the midst of unsettling and challenging change. It is our hope that in this book you will see rural life anew, and with gladness renew your commitment to be part of the community of sustaining life-givers, so abundant in rural communities.

Looking with the Heart: The Patchwork Quilt of Ministry

As in the patchwork of a quilt where the separate squares are stitched and interconnected to make the whole design, so the segments of rural culture and life are interconnected. The patterns of land, families, congregations, family farms, alternative movements, grassroots organizations, outreach services, town centers, and more are sewn together into a design of spirit and heart unique to what is described as *rural*. The making of quilts has been a communal part of the history and customs of the people and continues today in many homes, churches, and organizations in the Midwest. The heart is a fitting symbol for the so-called "heartland" that names this central portion of the United States. Heart represents the hospitality, close relationships, courage, and commitment that can be found there. In the layout of this book, it seems fitting, therefore, to use the image of a quilt with squares and hearts representing the special segments and spirituality of this rural culture, stitched together to make one whole in the heartland.

When one segment of a quilt tears away or unravels, it affects the design and unity of the whole. Such is true of life in the rural Midwest. With the rapid disappearance of many family farms and their unique way of life, we see the sustainability of churches, communities, and organizations threatened with this unraveling. This book seeks to find a way to sustain the spiritual heart of rural people in the heartland. Explore the culture, spirituality, and warmth of heart in this vital yet challenged segment of rural America.

Using This Book

This is a book you can approach and reflect on in many ways.

- We encourage all readers to begin by browsing. Flip through to get a sense of the organization and then to find what connects with you immediately. It may be a chapter in Part Two about a particular rural group or patchwork piece *you belong to*—family, town, institution, church. Find yourself in it. We hope you will realize in a fresh way your contribution and importance to the rural whole. Notice that there are nine other such chapters structured in a similar way and describing the contributions, challenges, and spiritual generosity of others in your rural world. As you look at those chapters you may see people around you in a new way and begin to appreciate your community companions with their spiritual intentions, their seasons, their special piece in the rural patchwork quilt.
- Pastors, lay leaders, or networkers may move directly to the ministry suggestions, looking for sensitive and practical ideas. Each chapter of Part Two ends with suggestions for pastoral response, and Part Three includes a summary list of pastoral strategies. Once you have the sense of Part Two, you may want to skip around, or save

some chapters for when you plan to connect with some people represented by those chapters. However, a full read will open you to the many dimensions of your rural world you may not have given much thought to. There is a helpful *Resources Two* section at the end that contains prayers and rituals for many occasions.

- Pastors, seminarians, lay ministers, as well as sociologists and educators will find the fullest meaning through front-to-back reading. The text gives an experiential and spiritual point of view not common to much exposition about rural life. It also interweaves research and reflection of theologians, sociologists, teachers, and official church leaders responsible for rural ministry. It illustrates chapter by chapter that the notion of "rural spirituality" is not all of a piece, but is manifest in special ways by each group. That is important. Part One describes characteristics and themes of rural spirituality and adds an interesting connection of rural conversational talk to possible rural theological or God-image understandings. Part Two describes the roles, dynamics, spirit, and challenges of ten groups in the quilt of rural life. Part Three adds dimensions to the picture of rural church. We found rural spirituality not to be self-conscious, but rather down-to-earth, responsible, interconnected, challenged, and generous. Notes provide further information and ways to make contacts.
- Some will notice that each chapter in Part Two begins with a story and will appreciate the personal approach to the text. Within each chapter are real experiences of heartland people and notes at the end that often give more description. There is also a full section in *Resources One: Lectionary of the Seasons* that uses stories for reflection.

All readers, rural and urban, will take heart, for there is heart and spirit in the heartland, and the church is in the center as gatherer, sustainer, healer, participator, servant, and leader.

CHAPTER 2

RURAL SPIRITUALITY

A committed and experienced ecumenical group of about forty, clergy and laity, came together at the invitation of the Churches' Center for Land and People and the Center for Theology and Land to reflect on rural spirituality and implications for pastoral ministry. In small mixed groups they considered first "What is spirituality?" Sharing insights, the entire group then reconvened to get some common understandings. Back again into small groups, they then considered *rural* spirituality, its special experience and expression. In a last round, ministers and laity met separately. Ministers were to consider what they wanted to understand better about the people's experience of faith. Lay members considered what they would like those in ministry to understand better about their rural lives and their expression of faith.

This session gave the impetus for work that has become this book—an effort to describe the rich ways spiritual life is formed, expressed, ministered to, and shared in rural America. Five years of exploration in a wide variety of interactive settings has enabled us to see and to honor the rural character of faith. We share this to help pastors and lay leaders understand, support, and strengthen their members. And we encourage all people of faith in the heartland to embrace their life's call in these stressful times of change and diminishment affecting families, farms, churches, and communities. This and the rest of Part One are beginnings. They take flesh in Parts Two and Three.

What Is Spirituality?

Christian spirituality may be described as the way that Christians live out their lives with God, neighbor, and the world by the energy of God's grace in Christ. This suggests an integrated vision of person, vocation, church, and community, within the whole living creation. Spirituality is related to awareness, mystery, attunement to the divine context, what makes us yearn, and what gives our life its deepest meaning. It acknowledges our dependence on God, puts us in touch with the holy, calls us to be for others, and moves us toward what is life-giving. It is expressed through prayer, a disciplined faith-full life, and through just, compassionate relationships with others.

Healthy Christian spirituality depends on our sense of who God is and how God relates to the universe and the human community within it. God-images of a creative, loving, just, and nurturing God—such as Christ expressed—shape us as persons created in that image. A growing spirituality deepens in gospel values: love for God and neighbor; respect for God's creation; faithfulness; truth-telling; sharing of life; care and advocacy for the poor; joyfulness; and a lifestyle of peace, mercy, and justice. Challenges to Christian spirituality are found in our empty consumerism, possessive and violent ways of protecting what we regard as ours by right, and extreme individualism. Such problems are amplified in our culture's striving, and in our fast-paced, pressured life. Churches are not immune to such societal pressures. As is true in every age, gospel values are challenging.

What Is Rural Spirituality?

Rural spirituality has a distinctive spirit. It is a spirituality of land and relationships—a spirituality of the heart. It is filled with commitment to stewardship and to connectedness generation to generation. It is a faith from both Christian tradition and lived experience. Is rural spirituality the same as urban spirituality? Faith is at work, as in the stories below, but it is expressed in ways particular to rural attitudes, relationships, concerns, and call.

> A young family farmer, whose land was in the shadow of their local church for generations, said of their family efforts in the face of record-low prices: "*We have faith every day, and we believe that everything is going*

to work out, just like we believe every year with the crops that we will have a good season. It doesn't always work out that way, but we hope for the best and leave the rest up to God."[1]

Speaking at a Rural Life Gathering, a woman said of the choice she and her husband had made to "make do" with their small acreage: "*We have grown to see ourselves as stewards of the land, good-will ambassadors to the community, guides of the next generation, and advocates of the family farm.... We will be happy, have a sense of place, a true sense of family, and we will preserve and protect God's gifts for those who are yet to come. I find honor in that duty."*[2]

Steeped in churches' gospel-based teachings of social justice, a dairy farmer and activist speaks out against trade policies that have undermined the rural vocation and have globalized hunger and poverty in the world: *"Our vision of a just food system is to create rural economies based on self-respect, respect of the land, food sovereignty and fair trade."*[3]

Read reflectively the following characteristics of rural spirituality. Each is a gift received and a gift offered to the world:

- Appreciation of nature and its seasonal rhythms
- Reliance on the providence of God amid the uncertainties of life
- Rootedness in the land and community over generations
- Valuing the interrelationship of land, plants, animals, and people
- A sense of living in a covenant with the Creator; stewardship as vocation
- Focus on family kinship and cooperative relationships with others

- Awareness of the seasons of birth/growth/death/new life and acceptance of life as it is
- Belief in making a contribution to the world
- Responsibility to coming generations
- Growing commitment to act for justice
- Trusting that God will provide.

Pastoral Implications

Those in ministry learn to understand and value these special lenses and strengths. National church resources tend to reflect urban perspectives and problems. Although there are numerically more rural/small-town churches than urban/suburban ones, the great majority of members of mainstream churches live in urban or suburban areas. Because rural ministry is not just an urban ministry with cows and crops added, the programs and resources from church offices may not always be a good fit for rural/small-town settings. Thoughtfulness on the part of rural pastors, teachers, and lay leaders will connect the gospel to the rural way of life and the issues of concern to country and town parishioners.

Actually, many of the Scriptures are expressed in creation metaphors and community settings akin to the rural milieu. But urbanization is impacting many in the rural community, leading to dissatisfaction with traditional values, especially among the young. In addition, the gifts of rural spirituality listed above are disregarded and even denigrated by a corporatized agriculture with its competitive pressures to get big at any cost, or get out. The great tragedy of heart in the heartland is that when farming is reduced purely to economics, families are robbed of their most fundamental sense of vocation. As the farm crisis deepens, anger, depression, loss of meaning, and sense of powerlessness fill the countryside with hidden pain. The rural community asks: Where is God amid all these things?

Parts Two and Three of the book explore ways to appreciate and support people of spirit active in rural communities today. Rural churches and pastoral leaders are important as they reach out in the rural community that is working to define its place in a changing world. They will offer resources rooted in spiritual wisdom and appropriate to the realities of rural life. They will work with the communities to realize their inner strength to recover their spiritual balance and move forward with vision and hope.

CHAPTER 3

THEMES IN RURAL SPIRITUALITY

A number of themes become clear in most discussions of rural-life realities and spirituality today. We found these can be named in terms of: living the seasons; conflicting values/directions; chronic farm crisis; stewardship of creation; gift and vocation; relationships and community. In many conversations biblical, theological, and pastoral perspectives surface spontaneously in both laity and clergy, though a bit differently. It suggests there is an age-old, deeply felt integration of faith and life in rural people. There is a similar sense of faith and life connection in rural pastors but in a more trained and ministerially conscious way. Both perspectives are shared here.

Seasons of the Rural Year

Rural people are highly attuned to the seasons. Ben Logan's classic *The Land Remembers* tells the whole story of the author's growing-up years in a Wisconsin farm family in the framework of the seasons. People match their work, celebrations, and sense of life to these changes in creation. It is in their bones; they *know* how to live and move and have their being in God's natural world. The annual round of work with the soil, animals, and crops is a fruitful source of spiritual learning and worship: "It's what my heart tells me to do; it helps me in my faith, and restores my joy. I feel God's presence."[1] Although rural people may describe their moods and setbacks in terms of weather (cold, dry, stormy), they often relate their positive experiences in terms of the seasons: harvest (joy, pride, fulfillment); Thanksgiving time (bounty, grace, gratitude); late winter (rest, waiting, yearning); seed time (freshness, excitement, new beginnings); and growing season (nurture, hope, future).

> *Rural churches often symbolize the seasons in worship. It is good to build on where the natural seasons and the liturgical calendar coincide as revelation of divine mysteries. We can strengthen that powerful connection through Scripture, music, poetry, visuals, and special prayers or rituals.*

Clash of Values

Just as not all urban people think alike, not all rural people think alike. There is a wide range of experiences and points of view. In the rural community today there are a number of recurring conflicts, a basic one being choices in how to farm—traditional/conventional, industrial, or alternative.[2] What an individual decides is considered a choice in values. "Dad could have made more money with conventional farming like everyone else," a young man said about their alternative way of farming, "but he felt that a farm has a direct relationship with people, whether those people are here today, tomorrow, or fifty years from now."[3] Interpreted in terms of values, choices increase the sense of judgment or criticism when those choices vary farm to farm and can in effect divide people.

Many differences and opinions are "inherited." Because exposure to a range of other cultures and ways is limited in the traditional rural milieu, those differences, whether familial, cultural, religious, social, or political, can be taken for granted as the "right" way. This can make living in a small setting challenging. The new-to-rural/long-time-rural divide is classic and affects both community and church. The daughter-in-law marrying into the family and farm is another. Other conflicts may be liberal/conservative; economic competition/cooperation; youth/adult perspectives and values; biblical reference/social science orientation in dealing with life's hard realities. In rural communities of countryside and town, differences are felt close-up but are often dealt with obliquely to preserve a sense of harmony for the long term.

> *What insight and support may pastoral leaders (clergy and lay) offer to parishioners caught in such clashes? Rural life offers fertile ground for developing deep values, as well as for learning how to manage differences and keep relationships over many generations. Jesus often said, "My peace I give to you"* (John 14:27). *But he also said, "I have not come to bring peace, but a sword"* (Matt 10:34). *It may be beneficial and even necessary to provide opportunity for people to examine and evaluate the sources of their values and opinions. Being both pastoral and prophetic is challenging in the rural milieu where conflict is among people who know each other personally.*

Chronic Farm Crisis

The third set of themes relates to the harsh emotional cost of the economic "farm crisis" now become chronic: grief, anger, depression, despair. In the heartland, farms are being lost at an average rate of four to five farms a day per state. All family farms are supported by off-farm jobs. Long hours and low prices create immense stress, and put a strain on otherwise strong family and community relationships. "I have experienced such pain," a woman said, telling her story. "Our farm debt became insurmountable and we finally had to sell out. I was left with a crushed spirit. Everything seemed impossible. I struggled to put my life back together. Eventually I knew I would make it, but it took Jesus walking with me every step of the way, continually reminding me that 'nothing's impossible.' "[4] When people talk about themselves, their families, neighbors, and community members, the catch in their voices and the pain in their eyes says it all.

> *We search for pastoral responses to very hard questions. Where is God in the midst of pain? Is our church and community's faith strong enough to hold both loss and hope at the same time? How do we respond to those in need? What is the "Good News"? These are ageless human questions; ready answers will not help. But relationships can. And skilled pastoral*

care can allow faith-struggle to go deep enough to yield and cry for help.

Stewardship of Creation

Respect for the land and a sense of earth stewardship are at the center of the being of rural people. Families will describe with pride what improvements they have made over the years on their land, their efforts to keep the water pure, their love of the animals. The psalmist says the earth is the Lord's, not ours. The Hebrew Scriptures are filled with affirmation: the goodness of creation, food given and shared—fruit of the earth and work of human hands. "It is a sacred act to break bread together," a gardener said. "It is a recognition of Jesus in Emmaus and around every table; where we eat we reconnect with the human experience and our dependence on God."[5]

Rural people recognize God's expectation that humans will take good care of these gifts (Gen 2; Ps 8) and live by the gospel teachings that emphasize the redemptive, recreative, and just work of God who is making all things new (Rev 21:5).

> *We might use the Scriptures we know so well to deepen people's spiritual connections and to honor their faithful stewardship. God called the creation good* (Gen 1) *and blesses the land for those who work it. God has a purpose within all creatures, and we are part of God's continuing presence in creation* (Ps 139). *The earth suffers often at our hands, and will rejoice when we return to our God-given vocation* (Rom 8; Isa 35). *The heavenly bodies and living creatures teach us about God and life* (Ps 104), *if we have the eyes to see and the ears to hear. In fact, the whole created order works with the just and turns to desert at the hands of the unjust* (Ps 107). *The Sabbath and Jubilee* (Lev 25) *reestablish right relationships and rest for land and people.*
>
> *Many of the parables were based on Jesus' close observation and appreciation for the whole creation. God cares about small birds and lilies* (Matt 6), *farmers*

and fishermen, the poor and oppressed. Christ taught the way of harmony and relationship. The reality of death and resurrection, which farmers know well, are at the very center of creation and hope. In Christ we can begin again (2 Cor 5).

Gift and Responsibility

Over and over the people who participate in exploration of rural spirituality speak in terms of blessing and responsibility, of being part of God's plan, of working in faithfulness to a deep-seated call. They have a highly aware, though humble, sense of vocation in regard to family, land, and community. "My husband and I are farming on the farm of my parents, grandparents, and great-grandparents. I have immense responsibility to the community of the past, present, and future to care for that soil."[6] Rural experience and life wisdom are one with their Christian faith.

They also recognize with respect and gratitude many companions in spirit who, though they may not be explicitly churched, share a true commitment to the same work and a sense of call greater than themselves. The call is to stewardship, relationship, and justice. This sense of vocation must be nurtured today because the pervasive language is not spiritual but economic—management, competition, bottom line.

It is good to honor and reinforce this sense of call. We are dependent on God's sustaining power and blessing. Created in the image of God, we are called to participate in God's loving creative purposes. The call to responsibility (dominion) in Genesis invites us to stewardship and partnership with God, yet some have seen that call to mean domination. Our failings entangle the rest of earth's creatures in our cycles of disharmony and destruction. As a gift of the Spirit, hope moves us to envision a new day, to participate in the creation of a new heaven and a new earth. Christ manifests the divine energy of love which not only "moves the sun and stars" (Dante), but calls us to do our part in bringing forth life. "Whom shall I send?"(Isa 6:8) *Rural people say, "Send us."*

Relationships and Community

Finally, it is clear that at the heart of rural life is relationships, and central to people's understanding of Christian tradition is community. Every day, despite their pride in being rugged individuals, rural people of town and country know they are interdependent and rely on daily and lifelong commitments of family, neighbors, and community. "If we are going to sustain the world," we are reminded, "our hearts are important and we must remember we are not alone."[7]

> *In this time of social fragmentation, perhaps because of it, people are beginning to see how God loves us as a people. It is a great spiritual strength that rural people are naturally communal. The love within the Trinity is relational—abundant, interactive, and missional. Thus spiritual growth always moves out beyond self to others. Rural people do that. God formed the Israelites into a community of faith related to the land and responsible to each other in love and justice. In good times and in bad, everyone is important, cared for, admonished, responsible: a chosen people choosing God together.*
>
> *Like rural people, Jesus was grounded in place and community. He began his ministry in the setting of a family and community celebration* (John 2). *Every day he was among the people and their concerns. When he saw that they followed him "like sheep without a shepherd," he "had compassion for them" for their discouragement* (Mark 6:34), *and taught them their real importance in the eyes of God. "Blessed are the poor in spirit, the meek, those who hunger and thirst for righteousness..."* (Matt 5). *He modeled for them how to give from the little they had (five loaves, two fishes). In sharing, they found there was more than enough for all* (Mark 6). *At Pentecost,*

the Spirit of God—Counselor and Advocate—poured out among them "many gifts" for the good of all. The early Christians, not unlike rural communities today, understood that relationships are the basis of the common life, where all is shared, all risked together. Together we are "filled with all the fullness of God" (Eph 3:19).

CHAPTER 4

HEARING THE HURTING HEART OF RURAL AMERICA

Rural culture is an oral culture. Ideas, feelings, and a sense of relationship are experienced through news-sharing, conversational debate, common expressions, storytelling, shared jokes and songs. In personal or family hard times, the talk gets strained, and the sense of relationship among themselves, others, and with God diminishes in the silence. A key to ministry in the rural culture is to listen and to listen caringly, with a spiritual ear to spoken clues of hopes, struggles, theological understandings, and faith. Stories received and held in God's love can breathe new life and hope into the persons telling them.

Today's economic and social powers fill media and advertising with the language of business, as though marketing and competition were the only ways to describe "the real world" in the global age. Faith frames reality in spiritual dimensions that grow out of biblical and theological understandings of unity and justice. It is critical to keep the language of spirit alive, and to tell stories that connect rural people to God, one another, and the land in a way that will revive their hearts in times of crisis, embolden their action, and renew their sense of identity and vocation.

These are confusing times. Listen to people's hearts—the assumptions, heartbreaks, and hopes that underlie their words. Their language reaches out to be in touch, to seek response. Here are some of those short sentences revealing vulnerability, seeking something. Do not let those words slip by without your holding them gently in the presence of a loving God. There will be a time and a way someday to speak spiritual truth that sets them free.

"I guess I'm just not a good manager."

Today when farmers are in losing situations they are likely to say what they have been told by agribusiness to think: that it is their fault, that they are poor managers. The old "rugged individual" concept does not serve them well when it puts them on their own, as though they were personally and totally responsible for what is not thriving on their farms. Further, the business accent on competition separates people from one another. This new kind of isolation is deeply felt in families and communities today. We as a community of faith hold forth a different vision that includes compassion and unity. We must speak in such a way that people can see more clearly that rural loss today is not personal failure, but due to a system intended to reward the "big." There is need for healing, yes, and for protest.

"If I just prayed more...."

This is a lament—confusion in the face of defeat. It also reveals a God-image that is not true or helpful. Assumed or unconscious connection between a person's spiritual effort and God's favorable material response only distorts and troubles, adding a further burden of guilt and unworthiness to people already in pain. When God is seen as judge more than as redeemer or life-giver, the person concludes that God is not only absent, but even displeased when times are bad. Economic reverses feel like disinterest, or worse, punishment from God; and conversely, economic success can feel like reward for one's hard work. It feels as if the responsibility is on the individual to measure up to the requirements of God—to "pray more" or to do more of whatever one thinks is "spiritual." This also robs the person of the feeling of joy at receiving God's grace and love as gift because it feels only earned. The ministry of the spiritual guide is to deepen awareness of the unconditional love of God for each one regardless of economic state, personal situation, or ability to fulfill what are perceived as requirements for receiving God's love and blessing.

"When we get things together, we'll go back to church...."

The sense that they are responsible for everything themselves distances people from the help they need when there is loss. Shame or anger keeps them away from the church and their community of faith. Listen for what is underneath the words, the unspoken sense of alienation: "We are alone. Where is God's love for us? Doesn't God care about justice for farmers? What are we doing wrong? Where is Christ in our darkness?" If there is no spiritual intervention, the grief over economic/personal losses translates as abandonment. The downward spiral can move people through anger to depression and despair. The minister and community must reach out, yet allow space for privacy and healing. This is a ministry of attending to and helping people to sort out their feelings, find their reserve strengths, and then to connect with community and state resources. It is a sensitive matter to try to bring spiritual insight too quickly into their pain, as though there were an answer to suffering. A spiritual guide may reflect with the person on their story within the frame of God's compassionate love and the mystery of Christ whose suffering became our source of hope, but only over time, and prayerfully. Congregationally, it may be time for attention by the churches and community to larger systemic issues.

"I love this place. This farm (or local business) means everything to us."

These words, when spoken in good times, express people's deep and proud connection with the land and community. Because farm families so identify with their land and their stewardship of it, these same words, if spoken when facing loss, carry great sorrow, and even anger. The same is true of people with local businesses, also passed down in the family, who are faithful contributors to the community. If the farm or business "means everything to them," then who are they if they are losing it? What is their worth? What else can they do? This loss of meaningful place in the world is a spiritual crisis to which we must be very present. Rural people have already been disconnected from their spiritual selves by a world that names everything in economic terms and sees their crisis only in terms of efficiency: "Just sell the farm or business and do something else." The spiritual responses again are to challenge the model that reality and meaning are only economic, and to nurture the natural spiritual sensitivities of rural people. If there is loss, much work must be done to help people realize that their deepest identity is as children of God, loved and worthy. And to know, if necessary, that they will be capable of moving on to another kind of meaningful life, carrying with them the special gifts that have been given to them. This recovery of spiritual wholeness over time can give them new visions of what God's grace can do with their lives and livelihoods.

"The pressure is getting to the whole family, and our neighbors are too busy to visit."

The breakdown of family and neighborliness in the face of stress causes great loneliness for family and community-oriented rural people. Families are deeply weighed down when stress and multiple obligations come to dominate in their hard-working team. They lose the rewarding sense of all working the land together and the camaraderie of family talk and play. Spouses, with one of them often working off-farm, have little time for each other. Children's needs may be neglected. And sadly, youth begin to look at the situation and choose not to remain on the farm, but rather to try and find employment that seems less stressful and more personally rewarding.

Furthermore, neighborly relationships break down. Few have time for conversation over coffee or a shared project. Even though the legendary response of working together to help a farmer in sudden need still exists, this generosity of spirit is diminished in the increasingly controlled and competitive agricultural system. Trust may be replaced by suspicion about a neighbor's intentions when one farmer's loss could mean a neighboring farmer's gain. The pastoral call is to rebuild community where it is in danger of disappearing, to support families, and to offer hope to those at risk of losing their livelihood. And pastoral care should include watching out for the effect of family stress on children and teens. Ways should be found to give couples a break. The language of community and common good should be kept alive.

"I haven't talked to the pastor, and no one from the church has talked to me."

Rural people are private and do not let others, even the pastor, know their troubles. Yet they want the church to respond.

To honor privacy, rural churches may be reticent in offering support. Or they may be conflicted because in small communities the lenders and seed sellers are in the same congregations as the borrowers and planters. Yet the church's help and respect is needed. Silence causes additional pain, and people who are hurting may drop out or drift away from the faith community that seems to have little to say to them. By not supporting rural people in their struggles, churches seem to endorse the idea that God is interested only in those who are successful. Sometimes rural pastors may not know how to bring the resources of the Good News to bear on these struggles. Pastoral leaders, both lay and clergy, need to build bridges of trust between churches and families. Parish nurses can be helpful here because they have a reason to visit, are trained in pastoral listening, and represent the church to the people they visit. And once again the church may be called to speak up for those who have no voice when a prophetic word is needed.

"Our church never does anything."

There is congregational God-talk in time of stress as well. When members of a rural or small-town congregation describe themselves as "never doing anything," they may be using the traditional self-effacing expressions common in rural culture. Unconsciously, they may compare themselves to "thriving" urban parishes whose organized and assertive ways are quite different from the unfolding and relational nature of rural churches. Today it is important that pastors and congregational leaders listen carefully for distress beneath these statements and work to build up the spirit and spiritual power of their members.

Looking at the congregation's past and present life can be a springboard to celebrating and then reenvisioning the future. A church mission or retreat can gather the people for a storytelling review of the history of their congregation. It is a church that has remained faithful all these years, has its well-known leaders and saints, has been a long-term stable place in the community. Besides celebrating the past, it is important to help the church assess where it is alive in the present. Cultures and theologies have changed since the earlier times of more insular church communities. Today we think in terms of outreach, sharing the Good

News, working with other churches, being a part of the public life of the community. When people imagine they are doing nothing as a congregation, they should be encouraged to experience everything in their lives as being church. That is where they bring their faith, where they build up others' hope. What community organizations are they involved in? Where do they volunteer? Where do they contribute to the community's welfare? What roles do they take (as Jesus did) as teachers, healers, leaders, advocates? Making the link between the power of their faith and the generous spirit they share in the community will help to open their eyes to how truly active they are.

"We will hang on as long as we can, then close the doors...."

Some small rural churches with aging parishioners, declining numbers, and no regular pastoral services in place may give up any hope for a future. That may be a realistic assessment, but it could also be a self-fulfilling prophecy unless a new attitude begins to turn things around. Nostalgia for a happy past can crowd out present experience of God's love or the hope that we always have in Christ. It can also block out seeing other possibilities God may be calling the parishioners to. Many congregations today are finding ways to share with others. Some are merging so as to strengthen the worship, religious study, and community. Congregations are called to affirm life, even in the presence of death. With God all things are possible, even resurrection.

PART TWO

The Heartland: Vibrant Quilt of Relationships

A rich way of coming to understand and honor rural life and spirituality is through the image of a patchwork quilt. The intricate colorful patterns, the careful stitchings, and the overall design represent the interconnected relationships that are the heart of rural life.

Part Two is about those patterns, those relationships. This is the heart of the book, highlighting chapter by chapter the land and people that make up the living fabric of America's heartland. After Chapter 1, "The Land," you can move from pattern to pattern in the other nine chapters in any sequence. The chapters describe the roles and contributions of each group to the whole. They point out the particular challenges they face every day in the changing rural world. The chapters describe their work, their spirit, their pain. And most important, they make visible their particular offerings to each other, to their communities, and to the world.

This section asks the people of the heartland, and those who serve in rural ministries, to notice ("attention must be paid"), to honor, and to give support. These are trying times. The planet and we cannot afford to lose this rich and strong heartbeat that offers its life-giving gifts day after day into the rhythm of God's creation.

Chapter 1

THE LAND

Soil and Spirit

The language of spirituality, the language of awe (which is in fact worship, humility, praise, and love) is rare in our practical, bottom-line world. Sometimes we are shy about using the language of awe and spirituality, even among ourselves in the faith community. The Spirit is moving us to let go of that reluctance. It is not just accidental that land-based groups are growing, that rural organizations create conference themes such as "Reclaiming the Sacred in Farming and Food," "Holy Soil, Common Ground," "Spirituality and the Land." This is not just "soft stuff." This is a moment in time—both a desperate moment and an exciting moment: a *call* all around the globe for land-spirit connection and to transformation of our ways of being part the earth.

I Am of Here

I am of here.
Here is of me.

When I stand on the land,
I feel myself as a brush stroke
of the earth swept into my being.

My life and family are a groundswell
of this place.

It has raised us, formed us.
Our life's rhythm breathes with the
rhythm of the land.

I am of here.
This land is alive.

I feel it in the wind that kisses me
with spring's awakenings,
warms me deeply with
summer's intensity
and nips me
with winter's sharp edge.

I feel it with the people that are my
family far beyond my family.

I am of here.
Here is of me.

Jan Libby [1]

"I Am of Here"

The poem says so much. When the urban teenage niece of an Iowa farmer rode along on the tractor, she asked her uncle why he farmed when it was such hard and demanding work and there was so much to worry about. Ambrose Koopmann stopped the tractor in the middle of the field to answer. Pointing to the east he said, "Look. Look at the land, the beauty—creation." They both took it in. Then he pointed south...west...north...each time pausing so they could appreciate the contours, colors, and scents, the freshness and growth, the wide sky and billowing clouds. "This is why I farm. You just have to pray when you're out here."[2]

The land is everything. It is beauty and challenge and satisfaction. It is also identity. Stop for directions to someone's home and you will hear something like this: "Keep down this road about a mile. As you come up the rise you'll see the Smith place on the crest of the hill—with the big maple in front. Watch for the turn on the right, used to be called Smith Road; I guess it's 126-something Street now. You'll cross a stream—well, it will be dry now. The second farm on the right with the big windbreak of pines is what you're looking for. Nice family, keep the land up, good farmers."

This gives a sense of the rural "geography of faith." Family, work, and spirit are formed by the land. Its shape and seasons get into the bones and its creatures allow your friendship. The land says to those who listen with attention close to prayer, "You are part of me." Revelation of the land's mysteries demands a lifetime of faithful relationship—generations—to learn to work with the intricate interconnectedness of its soil, water, seasons. But in that relationship, the earth is indeed "swept into the people's being" and they are blessed. A journalist wrote about the farm as a family member, a "living being" that provided a "pulse" many years for his family. "Ten Kliebenstein siblings share a common bond," he wrote in the *Tomah Journal,* "because of an eleventh family member, one we will miss when the time comes to finally say goodbye."[3] As the poem said, *"My life and family are groundswell of this place."*

"Here Is of Me"

The pastor visits, leans against the farm fence, walks down the lane with the young people and the dog to see the coming crops, sits down for coffee in the kitchen. There is pride, even in hard times, in what goes on here. There is a sense that "here is of me"—we have worked with the land, shaped its care, marketed its harvest. Whether the farm is thriving or struggling, the pastor can find the soul of the people very quickly. "You love this place." Their hearts open. "How long has this land been in the family?" The stories come, back and forth and around the table, the challenges and accomplishments, the family marks upon the land. "What has been your greatest challenge, and what do you like most?" The descriptions range poetic and technical: what they have done for beauty, how they have dealt with the water flow, practices that have enhanced the soil. This is the story of faith and stewardship. The pastor says, "You are really part of the land. Creation is still going on through you."

There is another way that "here is of me." These seemingly independent rural people form and impact a powerful web of interrelationships that give life and character to the wider community. The pastor asks, "Whom do you work with in this area?" The list gets long as they begin to name neighbors who help, a co-op group that shares ideas, the extension agents and fields days, the farmers market, the feed mill, the grocery store, and where they go for "parts." "Almost anybody," they answer with a laugh. "They help us, we help them!"

"It Has Raised Us, Formed Us"

The land has its seasons, and the seasons, to those who are attentive, teach the spiritual rhythms of life. There are times to be still as winter spreads purple across the sky and silence descends cold and clear. Churches enter the season of Advent, the season of quiet and waiting. Christmas births new life in the night and with it the grace of "ordinary time." Spring offers a burst of new song and the call to turn the soil and plant again. Always the seasons—seeds must die, new life comes, the Lenten Paschal Mystery teaches life, death, and resurrection.

The land has its ways—its contour, flow, diversity. It is not straight-lined. The land challenges the human desire for control with the earth's demand for give-and-take flexibility. The Spirit moves like the flight of birds catching the wind's current across the field. Pentecost, with bright flame and abundance—the many gifts—explodes our small mastery into mystery. *"Our life's rhythm breathes with the rhythm of the land."* "And God saw that it was good" (Gen 1:18).

"I Feel It with the People That Are My Family Far Beyond My Family"

The movement of earth-connectedness is happening all around the globe. At the same time that agricultural practices are more and more industrialized and food systems controlled by a few multi-national corporations, producers and consumers are awakening to the gift of food, the responsibility for soil, and the commitment to right relationship with all creation—in a word, to the sacredness of life, the holy space in which we live.

Rural communities are at the cutting edge of critical questions today. Who should control the land and the gift of food ("fruit of the earth and work of human hands")? How can the people of the world be enabled to feed themselves? How can we learn wisdom as humans in this living planet? What kind of future are we building for coming generations? We are indeed *"family beyond my family."*

The choices we make today are about spirituality and leadership. Similar to the Jews who fled the control of Egypt for the Promised Land, we are on the brink of a new sense of "landedness" where the decisions of what to do will be ours. In *The Land,* theologian Walter Brueggemann described that critical moment in Jewish history. Coming into land ownership meant leaving slavery and the wilderness and the taking on of responsibility.[4]

Call of the Land

Rural family, church, and community feel this call as privilege and responsibility. But increasingly their work with the land is described and evaluated primarily in terms of competitive place in the economy, efficiency, and bottom line. There is a painful disconnection from what is primary in their souls—the deeper wisdom, generosity, and sense of right—relations they have learned from years of stewardship and their genuine efforts to "feed the world."

The language of industrialized corporate agriculture is so pervasive that the church must be deliberate in its work to keep fresh for the people the language of sacredness and mystery, the privilege of their vocation to be caretakers of the earth and co-creators. The call of rural people—to honor the land, to work within the intricate web of creation and their own relationships, and to preserve healthy living systems for coming generations—is a sacred and awesome trust.

"See, I am making all things new," says our God of land and people. God makes hope possible, and newness is happening. Awareness is growing as many engage today's questions from a spiritual base. Groups are learning together new sustainable methods and forming cooperative systems for local and regional marketing. Around the country and world, in this "family beyond family," people are deepening their spiritual connections with the earth, creating rural-urban communities of mutuality and respect, and taking responsible action on behalf of quality of life and sustainable stewardship. We are here, people say, and we care about our lives together. The rural voice is strong. Like our parents and their parents, we are of the land, generation unto generation.

Chapter 2

FAMILIES

Story

John's folks truly believed and even hoped they would be the end generation of farmers. We were told that because the farm could barely support one family, if we wanted to farm, we would need to do so on a "volunteer" basis. We volunteered for the next eleven years.... We figured out that what truly made us happy was all around us, right there on the farm with our family, and that the farm needed to support itself. We kept our eyes and hearts on the goal and believed that if you perform worthy tasks you will live a worthy life. I cannot help but believe that the hardships and trials along the way helped to shape who we have become.

We started to rotationally graze as an economic-saving practice. What we gained was so much more. We gained: birds, natural habitat, happy cows, healthy cows, cows that live on our farm from birth to death (many over the age of fifteen), cows with names and personalities that are known and appreciated.

We gained: happy kids—kids that climb trees, kids that have their mom and dad as their teachers, kids that have their parents around, parents who know who their children are with and what they are doing (well, most of the time), and family meals that are a regular thing and not an event.

We give support to the community. We contract to local farmers for custom work. We volunteer in public service organizations. And we shop locally.... We are all connected to that land. There is so much life that comes from it. *JoAnn Pipkorn*[1]

Seasons Form the Rural Heart

In Scripture we read that Jesus came that we may have life and live it to the fullest. We could paraphrase that passage to read: Jesus came that we might know all the seasons of life, and reap the graces experienced in each season.

Rural families live the seasons. Spring, summer, fall, winter, are significant for far more than changes that affect travel conditions and recreational possibilities. For agricultural people the seasons are their life, the way they *are* in the world. They live in the rhythms—observant, ready, hardy, flexible. Working with the seasons demands attunement and judgment, knowing the time for planting, tending, letting go. They know the time for stewardship and they sense the divine mystery in the cycles and rhythms of nature.

This is not poetic. It is so real that most rural people rarely put it into words. To live with the seasons means to live with joy and unpredictability, abundance and drought, birthing and death. "The intense heat, blowing wind damage, flooding, downed power lines, and blizzards also gave satisfaction through our overcoming the burdens they inflicted," a farmer reflected as he thought of his family's experience. "The images of the extremes in weather, the broad realms of plant and animal life, and even death, the hands-on connection to everything—the farm family was a way to experience it all."[2]

There is unsentimental realism in rural people that frees them to do what needs to be done, and to enjoy what is meant for joy. The changes of the seasons are in their bones. This makes for hope with each planting, birthing, and proud harvest. It makes for caution because there is always the unknown, the fortune and ill fortune of weather and the market. It makes for humility because in the end it is God's work and God's mysterious invitation to co-create without control of all the elements.

For farm families who have learned the seasons, it means yearly gamble, and constancy for the long haul. This love and faithfulness is why farm families today continue to do everything possible to keep on farming. If they made it through the crisis of the eighties, they trusted the season would change. But in this continuing "drought" of prices below cost of production, with dwindling or no reserves, many have seen their land blown away by the winds of change.

Rural Family Living Is Communal

In the traditional way of rural living, farm families have opportunities to develop closeness that many metropolitan families do not have. Flexibility in time gives parents the opportunity to adjust chores for family participation and also to make time for freedom and fun. The land is central not only to work, but to recreation, with space for ball-playing, picnics, and afternoon gatherings. Land gives pause for reflection. Children learn to work hard and take pride in accomplishments. Everyone chips in to make attendance at special events, like sports activities and county fairs, possible.

Parents model involvement in community events and church activities so that children learn how to contribute. Even as pressures of time mount, the parents join organizations in an effort to affect farm policies and volunteer in local concerns and outreach. A child in school, when the class was discussing a particular national issue, piped up, "I'm not afraid of that. My mom is working on it!" That active mother, on hearing the story from her daughter's teacher, realized that "the magic of our hard work in instilling a little hope." How precious for the world. She added, "Look at the children around you—your work for justice, sustainability, or peace, right now gives them hope."[3] At home children also learn the holy rhythm of Sabbath. It is surprising in today's rushed and competitive world how many farm families observe Sunday as a time for a family meal after services, quiet time together, visits to relatives, and much-needed naps between morning and night chores. In all these ways, what remains constant is that the farm is a whole family affair and the children share the family values and workload as they grow into skills and responsibility. In this kind of togetherness, children learn to cope, to work things out, to give what they can.

The seasons of life—the work, play, worry, surprises, pride—are experienced together. As time goes on, the family team evolves with the growth of the children, the integration of the generations, and the interconnecting networks of kin. It extends naturally in the community of neighbors, business relationships, church, and community. Hard work and needs bring people together. The common good benefits all. In the community people give and receive as a family because they *belong*. They are saying to one another in many ways, "You really make a difference in our lives."

Seasons at the Kitchen Table

The centerpiece for the rural family in all seasons is the kitchen table. The front door of urban homes opens to the living room, but in rural homes the well-worn path is to the side door and the kitchen, with farm boots left at the door or "mud room." The kitchen table is central in the family's communications and transactions as one family member is grabbing up a snack before driving to work in town, another is heading out to chores, and another beginning to cook dinner. This is where news is exchanged and cares expressed.

In rotation each day the table sees the early-morning workers in from chores...the children collecting things for school...the couple working on bills, records, and plans...the county agent discussing a program...the pastor paying a visit...a neighbor stopping by to bring newly made jelly and to talk over coffee...kittens underfoot for a tidbit...the cousins in for an after-school snack...suppertime stories of the day...late-hour prayers to gain strength in the face of an uncertain future.

The table is central as the seasons change. It is the site of canning. Outside the children collect tomatoes or snap beans; inside the mother stirs pots and readies the jars. It is where the seasonal feasts are prepared. The members of the clan bring their favorite dishes and the children peek to see what they brought. The women gather in the kitchen in every season to talk about needs, relationships, school programs, sorrows, weddings, the new pastor, farm worries, and babies. For the men, the kitchen is the never-ending supply of cold drinks, popcorn, and chips for their games, and bantering talk. In the seasons of worry and hardship, the kitchen table is where they talk and plan and pray.

Disheartening Forces: Family Dimensions

For many farm families caught in ever-deepening economic depression, it is easier to identify with the seasons of hardship than seasons of celebration and abundance. A few years ago, many Americans watched the six-and-a-half-hour television documentary *The Farmer's Wife,* which depicted a young couple and their two children caught in a cycle of debt and overwork. Around the kitchen table, day and night, over more than a three-year period, their conversations weighed heavily with stress and fear. As they talked about food stamps, restructuring loans, and possible plans, they were too close to their own problems to see that the structures of big farming and corporate control were stronger than their individual energy and competence. In the film, no one, unfortunately, not even the church, asked, "Why is this happening to so many?"[4]

Similar scenes around family farm tables are all too prevalent. The family unit is stretched and worn thin. Like many people, a vigorous Minnesota couple in their forties, with three children of their own and a foster daughter, tries to do it all. Both Ron and Sue Visker work off-farm jobs and they try to stay connected to their community. But long hours take their toll. People say to Sue, "Oh, to raise your family on a farm—the quality of it." But she thinks, "What quality? For all of us to sit at a table and eat together, that's a rarity." The parents take turns going to the 4-H baseball games, take a one-week-a-year vacation away, don't have time to socialize. "We go to church, church functions. Mainly we're always coming or going. When people think of family farms they think of the Waltons.... Here, the stress level is unbelievable." Still Ron says, "This is all I've ever done. It's in my blood."[5] Another farmer observed that the family farm is traditional and farming itself is the tradition.

It is a tradition that means working together, working long hard hours in all seasons. Family members young and old work with complex farm machinery, chemicals, and large animals. They drive tractors, often old equipment, in rain and snow, late at night, on slanted land and country roads. Today's pressures create a syndrome conducive to major accidents: stress, isolation, physical fatigue, and interpersonal and social issues that can desensitize farm people to the dangerous environment in which they live, recreate, and work.[6] Add to this low prices, bills for ever-rising costs, and interest owed on loans, and all family members carry the strain.

Some family table circles break. The undercurrent of worry descends into hopelessness or erupts in anger, dividing the couple and deeply affecting the children. Necessary off-farm jobs take time from family and leave the members fragmented and exhausted. Many couples have become silent. The wife who works as the bookkeeper has to deal with her husband's resentment when there is not enough money for needed repairs and ordinary farm expenses. As the bills stack up it is not enough to farm fourteen to sixteen hours seven days a week, plus one or both working off-farm jobs. Depression makes it difficult to make decisions and increases isolation. Friends, neighbors, and even pastors hesitate to step in. Debt strains long-standing associations and business relationships. The local banker is in a tough spot and is likely tied by tight policies dictated by some distant head of the chain of the now consolidated banks.

The disappearance of farm families diminishes the health and interaction of the entire local community. Children travel distances to school and follow urban-oriented schedules that take them away from integral participation in the farm. They see their future away from the farm. Discouraged families withdraw from churches and other community groups. They are uncertain how to pick up the thread of faith and hope.

Family Choices

Concerns for "agrarian culture" are fundamental and even moral in nature. That is what Neil Hamilton of the Agricultural Law Center at Drake University in Des Moines wrote on the eve of the new millennium. "What happened," he asked, "to the values of being a good steward of the land, of nurturing livestock, of caring for neighbors, and serving as public citizens? If you search, you will find them in the tractor cabs, around the kitchen tables and in the coffee shops. But they are under siege and facing pressures like never before. With the drumbeat of 'advice' and predictions from business and the university, it is hard to maintain these values."[7]

Families are "choosing life" in many ways. Some, as described, are maintaining their farms by working in town. Many are taking risks of investment, perhaps buying more land by mortgaging the family home for the first time; or combining with others and incorporating; or taking out large loans to expand their operations short of "factory farming" and hiring workers. Some have given up their own farms and are working for others, receiving pay without the constant worry of management.

Many in developing their farms deliberately got away from chemicals into low-input sustainable farming. It cuts costs and along with good soil-building practices allows the land to come alive again. This change was suspect amidst the big promotion and seeming success of chemicals from the fifties to the nineties. One couple said that for several years they still pulled their herbicide and pesticide tanks behind the tractor—though empty—for fear of what neighbors would say if they appeared to be "going organic." They disposed of the tanks when they were sure the natural ways really worked! They also said it was their greatest joy when a few years later they were able to let their children play in the now safe soil.[8] Others found that rotationally grazing their animals made grasses last longer and provided good conversation time with the children as they moved the herds.

Coming new into rural areas is a movement of families who opt for a simple lifestyle in tune with the earth, many of them in gardening. They form networks to learn the ways of more organic growing, and interact with the community and urban neighbors. Some form CSAs (Community Supported Agriculture). They receive capital up-front from their shareholders for their seeds and work, and in turn supply these customers with fresh vegetables through the growing season. Urban and rural also come together in farmers markets.

All of these families value the farming way of life that keeps land and family life together. There may be conflicts about these different ways, but all are part of the quilt, securing "agrarian culture." When they come together in faith, they *know* what keeps them there. It is connected with their sense of God, family, land, and their call to do God's work.

Pastoral Responses: Sustaining Hearts

Pastors and congregations today must be able to respond in many different ways according to the seasons of their people. There are times to rejoice, times to mourn, times to build up, times to speak out, times to balance, and times to take sides. Pastoral responses will reflect all these seasons.

1. Families have learned how to maintain hope and stamina in times of adversity. They have also learned habits of privacy and overwork. Rural churches must know when to honor this strength and when they should offer help.

    - Trust builds when pastors and parish planners let farm families know they are important. Services must include prayers that address family realities, and rituals that recognize the special vocation of stewarding the land. Schedules for both adults' and children's activities should try to accommodate farm family distance and availability.

    - Be sure families know you understand what is happening in the agricultural economy and the pressures they are under. Read and listen to be better attuned. Friendly visits to their farms or kitchen tables over a period of time can build relationships strong enough to allow the visitor to know and touch their pain.

    - Studies show that church membership breaks down social isolation and keeps people connected and involved in the community. However, if a family stops coming to church because of hard times and depression, it may be well to encourage their return but not too insistently. Some need time and space to "drop out" for a while. Keep them in prayer and keep in touch, helping in any way you can. Listen carefully to the women and children. Help the children stay connected with friends.

2. One of the best ways to sustain hearts is to create ways for people to help each other.

    - Sandra Simonson-Thums, who herself lost her farm, has long worked in heartland states as staff for the Lutheran Church to respond to the rural crisis. She brings people together to talk to each other about their lives. They open the support meetings with a check-in. Often they begin with two questions: On a scale of one to ten, what level is your stress? Then they have a personal "weather report"—tornado, foggy, high pressure, cold front, sunny, partly cloudy. This gives everyone a chance to talk and is an indicator of who will need more time to talk that night. Over time it will also illustrate that in every life there is fluctuation, with times of critical need and times of good news. The first night of such a gathering, people need to talk on even to midnight. But afterwards they set a limit of one or two hours. They get better at expressing their feelings and become more sensitive listeners, getting past the usual "I'm fine." Sandra has developed a number of tools to help people identify their feelings: a Life Balance Wheel and a Rural Reality Survey. Often an outsider can facilitate the first meeting of these groups more easily than a pastor or congregation member, so search out help. Sandra also realizes that as more couples work off-farm, it is harder for them to find a time to gather. But after an initial meeting some have put together an internet chat room, or more simply, created an email list. They can do their "weather reports," exchange ideas, and give support.[9]

    - Send people to participate in programs offered in the area by other groups. Ron Hanson from the University of Nebraska-Lincoln was invited to a number of heartland states to speak on topics like "How to Thrive, Not Just Survive." One talk for young farm couples was on family farm communication. There was hot food, and the place was packed. With a twinkle he began, "Now you all know I'm not talking about you. It's your neighbor down the road I'm talking about." Everyone laughed. He was able to describe in humorous but accurate ways the intricate and often tense dynamics of intergenerational farming and give tips on how to handle situations.[10]

- The University of Wisconsin-Madison/Extension Health and Human Issues director, Roger T. Williams, offers workshops for rural area "helpers"—pastors, veterinarians, Extension Agents, social agencies, milk truck drivers, anyone who might regularly observe or interact with farmers. He helps them learn the signs of stress and depression so they can talk with the farmer or get help.[11]

3. Churches should know agencies and community resources available for families in need. Post hotline numbers in large print in the back of churches so people can see them easily. Have brochures with contact numbers ready at hand. Be both sensitive and practical in counseling.

4. Rural spirituality is an ethical spirituality. Rural churches and farm families must strengthen themselves for the ethical decision-making arena of today's industrialized global agriculture: cutting-edge issues of sustainability, justice, and life itself. Rural life today, far from being inconsequential, is where questions of healthy soil and water, bioengineering technology, and availability of healthful food are being lived out every day by farm families. Are churches there to help in this discernment?

   - An active church will include farm issues in their study of social concerns, and there will be church presence at meetings of organizations attempting to respond to unfair prices and controlled markets.

   - Use videos of *The Farmer's Wife* as an occasion of study together. The landscape that is hardest to see in this film is what we live in every day: cultural attitudes and assumptions, economic systems, and political understandings of power. To do justice to the struggles of the family farm we must look critically at this landscape because in a democracy the cultural/economic/political landscape is of our own making.

In this story, it seemed all up to the efforts of the couple, with no one asking *why* so many farms have been lost in America in the last twenty years. While the local parish was kind and offered counseling, there was no prophetic voice portrayed and no rallies or meetings about prices. We see a family with strong personal faith, but they must deal with the business language of management and efficiency. They suffer the minimizing of their true feel for the land and the experience of spirit.[12]

5. Honor your families because they are living their vocations at a critical time. Strengthen them in every possible way for their extraordinary journey. They have been called by God to cocreate the future. As a church we must be there with them as they accept this challenge with their traditional, generous determination.

CHAPTER 3

RURAL CONGREGATIONS

Story

In August of 1998 a severe storm lashed out in fury across the fields and towns of rural northern Illinois leaving a swath of destruction in its wake. Tall fields of corn were flattened. Trees were uprooted and broken. Grain bins, barns, and storage buildings were either damaged or destroyed by the high winds. With harvest nearing, it was a time of devastating losses for area farmers and ag-related businesses. The rural church was there to sustain the people in the midst of the crisis. A pastor in a hard-hit congregation chose to change the direction and theme of the upcoming Sunday worship in order to respond to the situation. The center of worship was structured to allow time for the people to lament, to name and grieve the losses they and many neighbors had experienced. Woven into the service was the assurance of God's presence, care, and concern as well as messages of encouragement and hope through Scripture, music, selected readings, and prayer. Conversation following worship indicated that hurting hearts were sustained by this prayer time together. They stayed after the service to organize ways to help. The congregation was sustaining hearts in the heartland. *Rev. Diane Jochum*[1]

In the Rural Landscape

All across the landscape of rural middle America one finds churches of varying sizes silhouetted on the horizons of open fields, nestled among rolling hills of grazing livestock, sprinkled liberally in the small towns and cities of the heartland. This idyllic scene of churches amidst thriving countrysides makes the more stark reality harder to detect. The truth is, there are fewer and fewer farm homesteads that once surrounded rural congregations. Instead one sees abandoned barns, or new large-stock operations and factory farms with confinement buildings, and Main Streets that are less busy. With the disappearance of smaller family farms and people moving away from the community, there often follows the disappearance of small rural congregations to sustain the spiritual life of those who remain. Yet the remaining congregations are symbols of stability and constancy, welcoming life amidst the chaos and pain of loss and change. How does one describe the heart of these remaining rural congregations?

The Heart of the Rural Congregation

The heart of the rural congregation beats to the rhythm of the Creator God's bounty of the seasons—processes of life, death, growth, and decay, including predictable cycles and unsettling unpredictabilities. It survives because its people survive with a tenacious optimism born of living with creation's potency and unfoldings, holding fast to confidence in God's sustaining grace. Rootedness spans generations, and the desire to sustain the intricate fabric of life runs deep. It is all part of a unique cultural identity.

Because many rural congregations are small it takes nearly everyone to help make something happen, especially bigger projects. Everyone plays a part. Church dinners, ice cream socials, and soup suppers are a celebration of breaking bread together. They enjoy the committee preparations and easy sense of camaraderie. It is common for people in a small area to support one another's events, and church fund-raisers are often ecumenically attended. In generous spirit families with gardens share their flowers for the altar and some bring their produce to put out after services. Sometimes donations for such produce are used by the church to support a particular mission, charity, or a need within the congregation, and what is left over can be given to local food pantries or delivered to homes of the elderly.

Thriving congregations are creative in worship, ministry, and mission within the framework of age-old values and identity. They are able to celebrate the giftedness of being small despite pressures to depend on numbers (of people, money, programs) to determine "success" as a church. They find ways to show respect for the land, its caregivers and stewards, and the rhythms and pace of rural life.

The rural congregation has rural neighborliness. People know and are known by name. Visiting together after worship happens naturally regardless of an established coffee hour. Extending a helping hand to a neighbor, whether church member or not, is part of the rural way. It finds expression in many ways—mission money given to a family who has recently birthed triplets, opening up space for a community meeting, providing a meal after a funeral. When a farmer is seriously injured in a farming accident, neighbors gather to finish the planting or harvesting, do farm chores in caring for livestock, and bring in meals to ease the family's stress. The congregation may organize a fund-raising event for medical costs.

Expanding Heart

Which comes first, church forming community, or community leading to the desire to pray and serve together as a church? In one poor rural area, a social worker serving with the people laid a warm community foundation. Called to a discussion about the area with his bishop, the Reverend Leo Maxwell Brown suggested that his Episcopalian diocese found a mission church there although the bishop had no money to spend on a building. "The church is the people that live there," the clergyman said. "We will build the community and church together." The social worker opened the basement of her home and she and Father Brown worked as partners. As the people offered care for one another, they began to express the need to worship together. That first Sunday of liturgical prayer in the small basement room, the pastor recalled that Jesus "created worship in makeshift places." A year later they built a simple church and the community and congregation grew along together.[2]

In most town and country churches, the community is far broader than the church membership. As congregational identity deepens, members must resist the temptation to turn inward. Reverend Carson Culver suggested to his two congregations that perhaps one of the things they could offer to the community was the service of their own pastor, time away from the parish to serve as fire and emergency chaplain. Later his service expanded to public office where he brings caring and ethical viewpoints to civic discussion.

The expansion of heart takes initiative, something rural women are good at. With twenty-five dollars from a "Seeds of Hope" grant from the Aid Association of Lutherans, two women set up a stall in the farmers market and hung up a sign announcing "ELCA Hunger Appeal." When they first began they brought irises and other flowers from their own gardens to sell. People asked about the sign, and soon others began donating gleanings and surplus produce from their gardens, even some baked goods fresh from their ovens. The two women who had shared their abundance made it possible for others to do the same. They received garden donations from sixteen local ELCA (Evangelical Lutheran Church in America) congregations, other denominations, and AAL (Aid Association for Lutherans) and Lutheran Brotherhood. The twenty-five dollars multiplied into more than three thousand dollars for world hunger.[3]

Parishioners sensitive to rural care and outreach in this difficult economy stretch their hospitality by working with other congregations and denominational staff in planning and hosting community forums on rural concerns. An Illinois presbytery of the Presbyterian Church U.S.A. created a Farm Family Task Force and applied for funding from the larger church. With a substantial grant, they began their effort to address stress and mental health needs. Planning collaboratively with other resource groups, they sponsored four ecumenical forums across the area. Each conference presented an economic overview, family life issues, and spiritual needs of the farming community to raise awareness and understanding in clergy and lay leaders. Agencies and organizations brought resource materials. Extension educators made presentations as did area spiritual leaders from the Rural Spirituality Project of the Churches' Center for Land and People. The shared meal prepared locally was important. The day was a beginning and created broad-based working relationships for the task force to continue its work.

Challenges

Though many rural congregations are tenacious and optimistic, there is no doubt the challenges are great. There are fewer people to draw on to sustain the congregation and its ministry. Many congregations face shrinking finances and people-resources to maintain ministry, building, and staffing requirements. With fewer young adults taking over family farming operations and more moving away for education or better employment opportunities, it is inevitable to see the graying/aging of some rural congregations. Although it is difficult, many of these smaller congregations collaborate, share a pastor, or even merge, denominationally or ecumenically, to provide stronger opportunities for worship, programs, outreach, and community. Providentially, in this time of challenge there is a rise in lay interest in church ministry and preaching. A schoolteacher explained, "I became tired of seeing our little church become smaller every year. We must depend on ministers who stay two or three years and move on. So I decided to do something about it." She enrolled in the Iowa Lay School, a program that grounds laity in solid theological education. She does not want ordination but simply to serve where she lives.[4] Most denominations have lay ministry formation programs.

Major changes in agriculture and marketing systems have brought sharp conflicting viewpoints. Many congregations face keeping the peace. There is strong division regarding agricultural, environmental, economic, and political issues. Some members have changed to contracts or larger operations to stay in farming, others have chosen to try to cut costs and stay with the smaller family farm, and still others are creating alternative methods of gardening and local marketing. All sit in the pews of the same congregation. Some may feel accused, others discounted, but most are sincerely just trying to make it. Adult Spiritual Formation sessions can bring people together to increase understanding and get to a deeper level of unity. Janet Kassel created an evening session in her small Catholic church. She invited a diocesan rural life director who himself raised hogs on a family farm; he had credibility both as a church spokesman and as a farmer. In the end, he could not come that night so

Janet, an alternative gardener (red flag for some) had to facilitate this delicate session. "It turned out fine," she said. "Everyone really tried to listen to one another. We do all care about families and farming."[5]

Differences between the old rural and the new-to-rural people also carry over into the life of a congregation. Urban/rural worldviews, ways of worship and programming, and styles of decision-making will collide. Differing hopes for the congregation, such as growth versus smaller intimate ownership, hamper a unified sense of identity and mission. Development of the rural landscape for recreational or suburban interests can be a point of contention. Hunting, fishing, and recreational access can be restricted in areas that were once free and open. Urban-suburban petitions for regulations on farm noise and odor feel like a challenge to the agricultural way of life.

Many towns now experience wider ethnic diversity. Workers from other countries, drawn there for farm work or the area's unwanted low-paying jobs, find it hard to fit into tight-knit communities and frequently meet with wariness and/or resentment. Communities and churches feel inadequately equipped to deal with the language, culture, and new social needs. Lutheran Pastor Dan Dibbert said he and his congregation sought common ground with the workers. Their church held a Hispanic commemoration, the celebration of Our Lady of Guadalupe, and brought people together in events that focused on culture, art, and foods.[6] With a nearby town, an organization was created named *Amigos de la Communidad*/Friends of the Community. In another state, Sister Christine Feagan, OP, who is fluent in Spanish, is director of Hispanic Ministry in a large Catholic parish. Much of her ministry is to welcome the newcomers and ease relationships in the town. She offered classes to some public school teachers so they could learn the basics of Spanish. She often acts as interpreter when families are facing complexities of unfamiliar policies or need appointments with lawyers, doctors, or other services. The parish does fund-raising for emergencies. She is a general resource to the community, talking with groups like the Rotary Club and Kiwanis, and is involved in advocacy as well. *Latinos en accion* was formed and is related to Iowa Citizens for Community Improvement.[7]

The Prophetic Heart

In this challenging time for rural America and rural churches, the prophetic voice of the church needs to be raised in order to address the disregard and displacement of farmers by national economic policies. The growing distance between farms and the impersonality of agribusiness make it harder for people to be neighborly. The economic depression has widened and deepened in small towns/rural communities and businesses. Sunday readings from the Lectionary speak of Jesus' love for the poor and his judgment of systems that oppress. There are many occasions throughout the liturgical year for relating justice themes to our times. The preacher is challenged to make clear these connections.

One who could do this very well was the Reverend Norman White, affectionately known as "Stormin' Norman." He began as rural-life director of the Dubuque Archdiocese during the farm crisis of the eighties, a crisis he saw deepen in the nineties. He was tireless for helping "hurting farm families." He combined pastoral care (bringing food and connecting people with resources) with prophetic denouncement of corporate systems. He gave spiritual counseling and led retreats; he would say he was fighting not only soil erosion but soul erosion. One thing he would do to spread his word about the plight of farms was to substitute at the Sunday Masses for any parish whose pastor was away. He found that urban churches were more receptive than rural. "Some farmers didn't want to hear it, and the powers didn't want them to hear it," he would say at church meetings. "This phenomenon makes it hard for a rural pastor to speak out." At Father White's death in 1996, Senator Tom Harkin of Iowa hailed him as a "caring, compassionate man, a tireless advocate for our family farmers, and a crusader for social justice."[8]

The pastor whose story opens Chapter 5 (Alternative Movements) found that when she shared with her church council what she learned about food-system concentration at a church conference, she was "set straight" by business members there. And her bishop, who wrote an open letter to his congregations with similar prophetic analysis, received a campaign of phone calls and letters saying the church had no right to speak on the economy.

The fact is, however, that mainline Christian churches have all spoken about agriculture through bishops' pastoral statements, assembly resolutions, and study guides that cite the Scripture and church traditions of social teachings. They speak for family farming as a better system for land care and sustainability, better for healthful social relations, and better for a just, shared economy. So Nebraska parishioner Annette Dubas called her pastor, the Reverend Richard Whiteing, to say "big pork" (mega-hog facilities) was coming to the area, and asked if he would come to a meeting. He had much to consider first. Where were all those statements when he needed them? He dug out a copy of the Economics Pastoral and called the National Catholic Rural Life Conference office for more materials. What about the fact that those involved (the Chamber of Commerce and the bank) were members of his parish? He studied hard. "The issue was more than political, more than merely about economics; it was about morality and relations between human beings." That Sunday he preached that the church must speak about these matters, that the law of solidarity and charity was clear. The phone calls began, the resignations, the threat of withdrawal of money, even from a distant Catholic high school, if that is what the church was teaching. But the people's confidence grew and grew, transformed from rural reticence to speaking out boldly to large gatherings in other communities facing similar threats. They formed Mid-Nebraska P.R.I.D.E., and as their work intensified so did the discouraging realization that the "big groups" hold the power. It is a great challenge. "They look more to the church for help," says Reverend Whiteing. That is good. Then he added, "But mostly they get silence."[9]

Pastoral Response:
Tending the Heart of the Rural Congregation

Tending the heart of a rural congregation can be as creative as one's imagination and as wide as the permission allowed and accepted within a particular congregation. The call is to both nurture and nudge.

1. The key to rural ministry is Presence. Office hours and programs are not effective. Join the rich and diverse happenings of your community. By listening in the natural contexts of your congregation's discourse, you will discover the relationships and networks that make up their lives. You will find their beliefs, gifts, and concerns. Rural culture takes a special kind of listening and learning.

2. Consider together what Judith Heffernan, executive director of the Heartland Network for Town and Rural Ministries, wrote: "Laity speaks to rural pastors: You're very important to rural families and to rural communities because you are often seen as the church...I do want to suggest two or three things to you: Lead us in powerful worship, powerful and relevant worship. We need to hear it. We need to experience it. Help us, maybe even teach us ways to shore up and deepen our own spirituality. Then, if you would, help us with this vision thing. In this country we have a vision war going on. It is a fight about what will be the compelling vision that guides us. The vision of what kind of community, what kind of society, what kind of family life we want....Most important of all to you who are clergy, be with us. Help us learn to be for each other what Christ would have us be."[10]

3. Celebrating the rhythms and changes of the natural and agricultural world is meaningful for farmers and townspeople alike. In spring ritualize the blessing of seeds, animals, and land, and have a commissioning of farmers and gardeners for their work during planting season. In the autumn, a harvest celebration will give thanks for the bounty. Farming is a physically dangerous operation: including prayers for the safety of farmers makes everyone mindful. Celebrate a Rural Life Sunday each year with earth stewardship emphasis. Because farming involves hard work and long hours, rural workers need reminding about the need for Sabbath rest and play to restore their souls. When tragedy strikes provide a special service of lament and prayers of hope. You will find some

rituals in Resources Two of this book, "Prayers and Rituals for Sustaining Heart."

4. In the administrative life of a congregation be attentive to the rhythms of agricultural life. Times of meetings, classes, special events, and weekly services affect the attendance of those who must do daily chores with livestock. It is helpful to avoid planning major events during the farmers' busiest seasons of planting and harvesting. Families would have low reserves of time and energy to offer for such events. Watch for the slower-paced seasons of agricultural life.

5. Support families at farm sales and auctions. Be attentive when farm families are suddenly absent from their pews or withdrawing from community life. Rural people tend to be private about personal and economic matters, not only for the sake of pride, but for protection in a small world where the banker or businessman might call in their loans or refuse further ones. Watch for the outward signs of depression and withdrawal. Sensitive support has literally saved lives. Kind presence and professional referrals may keep good and ordinarily strong people from feeling abandoned not only by their congregation, but by God.

6. Collaborate to offer events that showcase financial and social resources; send parish members to training sessions to learn active listening skills; send someone for parish nurse training; encourage participation on rural task groups.

7. Small churches can be reluctant to come together to write annual reports, especially for some located in areas of dwindling population and sparse resources. Assistant to the Bishop, the Reverend Kathy Gerking, suggests, "Why not make your own report form, complete with statistics *you* want to celebrate, and new categories that make sense in your context? Did you teach a child to sing 'Jesus Loves Me'? Did you go to visit that person who is mostly forgotten? Did you offer a word of encouragement or assistance to someone whose livelihood was threatened? The

greatest power is in the touch of Jesus, for it brings healing and new life."[11]

8. Study churches' social justice teachings on rural issues. Make these materials part of your preaching and available to your people. Invite preachers and presenters who can speak the prophetic word.

9. Churches are very important in a rural community. What churches decide to do, where they put their commitments, how they involve their members in the public life will affect the community for now and for the future. These are questions for the local congregation to consider in its reflection on mission.

    - How do you as a church respond to both the pastoral and prophetic call of the gospel within your community or area?
    - Do you encourage your membership to consider the consequences and contributions of their individual decisions in professional and civic roles for the quality of the whole community for now and the future? Do you honor them for this?
    - Is your church (ministerial association, judicatory) active in rural and community affairs? What kind of projects do you participate in or give leadership to?
    - What decisions are made (and by whom) when issues are sensitive or opinion divided in your membership of community? Can you identify a value or issue that your church embraced at a cost? How was it approached?[12]

10. Offer listening sessions to help people understand each other, even if they differ. What they have in common is that they are facing the same reality of changed agriculture and trying to respond in ways they feel will keep them in farming. The consolidated systems, not the individuals, are creating the context for difficult choices.

11. Avail yourself of denominational helps from the judicatory and national levels. Two such examples:

    - There are programs that facilitate reflection in light of church teachings, such as "Swine Production: Who IS My Neighbor?"—a process developed by the National Catholic Rural Life Conference that engages participants in considering various roles and views in a community in relation to right relations with others. Contact Tim Kautza: *ncrlc3@aol.com.*
    - A report and study guide, *We Are What We Eat,* was developed through nationwide rural grassroots participation facilitated by the Rural Ministry Office of the Presbyterian Church USA. It surveys the present situation of rural communities, offers alternatives, and recommends specific action for implementation. Contact Diana Stephen, Network Support, Rural and Small Church Ministries: *www.pcusa.org/evangelism/churchdevelopment/rm.*

12. Encourage lay education for ministry. Most denominations offer lay formation courses. One program, offered by the Center for Theology and Land, Dubuque, Iowa, combines online courses and residencies equivalent to about a semester and a half of seminary work. It is designed specially for lay ministers who seek to serve town and country congregations. Contact Rev. Dr. Shannon Jung, Director: *www.ruralministry.com.*

The rural church heart, like any other, is both strong and vulnerable. But consistently we find that there is warmth and wonderful growth awaiting those who choose to minister in a rural context.

CHAPTER 4
FAMILY FARMING

Story

Ask Gary what he does for a living and he will laugh. He is a farmer and a long-haul trucker. The corn he raises is seed corn for a big seed company and they consider him their employee. He must plant their way or no way. Gary has hogs, but because of truck driving he needs someone to look after the hogs, and so he is someone else's boss as well. Amid all this, Gary's wife works at the doctor's office, and between them they are raising two fine kids.

It is an amazing thing to consider how hard a family will work to stay on the farm. Gary wants to farm. It is his life. Gary's wife wants to be on the farm. It is her life. Gary's children have known no other life than that of winter, then planting, then harvest. It is their life. To stay on the farm, Gary drives his big rig all across the nation and his wife works long hours in the doctor's office. Their hired man spends more time on the farm than they do.

But stay on the farm, they do. I asked Gary why he works as hard as he does; he found it hard to answer. "It's just...." Gary slips into silence when trying to explain his feelings, and the sounds of the farm speak for him.

Sad to say, this farm will not see another generation of this family line still living in the house and working the land. Gary has filed for bankruptcy and will need to move. There is always the eternal hope of a bumper crop or an unexpected rise in prices, but the reality is that this will be their last year on the farm. The bills are too high, the resources too weak, and somehow the will of the farmer in Gary has been broken.

Still, in the cool of the evening, Gary stares out across his field and listens to the wind rustle through the corn and hears the land call. Ask Gary what he does for a living and he'll laugh. "I'm a farmer, I guess," he says finally with a shrug, and moves on to do his chores.

Then I heard the voice of the Lord saying, "Whom shall I send, and who will go for us?" And I said, "Here am I; send me!" (Isa 6:8) Rev. Tom Biatek[1]

A Tradition of Heart

You can't talk about family farming without talking about heart and about what it feels like to grow up on the farm: the sounds, smells, and rolling earth; hard work and family; neighbors, faith, and God. The family farm is about things being the right size—fields you can "walk" and work with, animals you can name and care for, chores you can fit to each age and talent as the children grow up, and satisfactions you can count in the family circle: pride, maturity, and bank account.

The tradition of heart is passed along generation to generation and is always told in story: how one learned to love the land and the skills needed to be part of it. As a teenager in high school, Leigh Ann Koopmann chose to write about her father when assigned to write about people who *leave footprints in our hearts*. "I'll never forget my first trip up the immense, blue, eighty-foot-high harvester with my tired, overworked, scruffy-looking daddy," she wrote. "It was the end of chore time; the hay was all chopped and the sun was beginning to set. He gazed at me and said, 'It's time you become a man and help your dad shut the harvester.' To a little eight-year-old tomboy girl, shutting the harvester and spending those few moments climbing it with my dad was more of a privilege than a chore. So up I went, huge step by huge step. I enlightened my dad at the top announcing, 'I'm a man now!'" Leigh Ann went on in her narrative. "He looked at his beautiful, precious daughter, chuckled and looked out across the land. I followed. It was breathtaking. I could see for miles. Now again a few years later my dad and I sit outside on the damp but soft grass, talking about what is wrong with the world today. Enjoying the memories we have shared together makes everything seem simple and for that moment all is right and the world is perfect. We both have our opinions, but I have noticed something—they are quite similar. Why? Because I know there is some of that great man inside of me shining through. He was the one that was in my life and left footprints on my heart."[2]

The Experience of "Call"

Family farming is a way of life. It is also experienced as a call, a special God-given relationship to the land, and the vocation to steward God's creation. A young farmer said, "When I'm driving my tractor out there, it's like—sometimes—I can glimpse God out of the corner of my eye."[3] Two women were filming corn harvesting in the bright Minnesota sun where "everything and everyone seemed ecstatic because of the perfection around us....The farmers were loquacious with the praise of the day, the harvest, the hawks and other beings around us. In other words, these men of the land were at home with themselves and their love of their work. They were in touch with *mystery.*"[4]

"Faith, family, and farm images were so intertwined," said agricultural agent Larry Tranel about his growing up on a farm, "that they all seemed to be one and the same." They determine his thoughts and behaviors now as an adult professional. "Growing up on a farm has shaped my vocation as a farmer, lay minister in the community, and University Extension professional working with farm families. Having our children and our marriage grow as part of a larger faith-filled community is what we seek." He reflects, "It is a call and gift to be a steward of the land and animals while helping to shape the community and world these children will grow up in realizing that God owns it all and has entrusted much to us as stewards in God's mercy."[5]

To hear family farm stories is to hear tradition and pride, resilience and vision. Every story is relational, with responsibility to land, neighbors, community, and far beyond. The mental framework of being the "bread basket for the world" is deep in the farm families' psyche. Farming is beyond making a living, beyond even quality of life. Farm families know, whether they articulate it or not, that what they do and the choices they make can make a difference to the world.

Season of Change

When we talk of family farms, we are also talking about the family farm *system* of agriculture. It is a system that has long provided quality products and genuine stewardship of the earth for future generations. It has also provided active community relationships and strong local economies.

But many family-size farms facing the industrial system of agribusiness today are squeezed out or forced to "get big" in the name of "efficiency." It is mastery, not mystery. In major heartland states the average income from farming is seven thousand dollars. Strong farmers are leaving. "It used to be that I couldn't wait to get out on that tractor during planting time," said an Iowa farmer who is in his forties and a past president of the Iowa Pork Producers Association. "For the last two years, all I've done is worry about how much it costs to put in a crop. I would worry that the price I was going to get for my crops wouldn't be enough to pay it all back."[6] Corporate clusters and mega-mergers control the markets and name the price. Accidents and suicides are the highest cause of death for farmers today.

"It takes a lot of courage to continue farming after what I've seen," Joel Greeno told participants in a CCLP Rural Life Gathering. "I've seen my parents' farm auctioned off on the steps of the courthouse: two hundred and thirty acres with two dairy facilities."[7] That is why this young farmer not only farms but works tirelessly as president of the American Raw Milk Producers Pricing Association (ARMPPA), building a national network of dairy farmers and helping to build local co-ops in order to be able to control their own price presently set by the United States Department of Agriculture (USDA) and for years set below the cost of production.

"For those holding on," says Keith Wold, who grew up on a family farm and served fifteen Iowa counties as a veterinarian, "the bar has been raised." Increased efficiency has brought increased stress in family lives. "I recently reminisced with a dairy couple that I had done veterinary work for twenty-eight years ago. I would come to do the monthly fertility check of their dairy herd. Afterwards, while the dairyman was finishing breakfast, I would have a cup of coffee at their kitchen table. Twenty-eight years later I reminded his wife of this as she was in the milking parlor attaching milkers to the cows. She said to me, with the voice and look of longing for what was, and the pain of what is, 'We eat very few meals in the house.'"[8]

The story opening this chapter illustrates the ways families have been stretched by off-farm jobs, structures of contracts, hired labor, and overwhelming bills. "Whom shall I send?" asks the Lord. The family farmers say, "Send me." But a market-driven world is not listening. Still, there are many like the veterinarian who have not given up. "I couldn't help but think," Keith reflected, "what a privilege it has been for me to have worked with these cows and their owners. Each animal had a special place in this farm's structure."

Hearing the Stories

To hear rural stories, pastors must get around to the family farms in their congregations, or to farm meetings in the greater area around their churches. As they listen they will find that stories differ from farm to farm, but that all are caught up in a major shift in agricultural systems, a shift that is bringing great pressures. A South Dakota pastor said, "Yesterday I visited with five farm families, and each one was either in a state of transition, or has left the farm, or is in a state of crisis."[9]

Some of the stories will describe endings after generations of skilled and faithful stewardship. They are worn down by years of high costs and economic depression, and low returns for every commodity. Families will tell of past accomplishments, family gatherings, hard times, and always another spring, but that this time the spring planting may not come for them. Receiving these stories is important, affirming both the realism and grief. While some families will be able to talk of pride in a job well done, their call accomplished, and the time to "turn it over," others caught in these changing times will feel failure, bitterness, or loss of personal meaning. They will feel cheated of their vocation after faithful years of working the land. They will need care, and perhaps professional referrals.

Other stories will be about continuing to farm. They will describe plans, struggles, adjustments, hopes. Some people are enlarging their operations while trying to hold on to their ingrained sense of good stewardship. Advised to double their dairy herd size, the Scheider family in Illinois studied and prayed and decided to take the financial risk. Speaking at a tri-state church-sponsored conference, they shared their Mission Statement. "Scheidairy Farms will produce high quality milk in a profitable manner in an environment wherein all people and animals will be treated with respect. We will be known in the community as being a progressive and compassionate organization. Those who observe us will recognize us as being committed to God in our daily lives, an employer of choice, and as environmental stewards. Our work environment will convey our mission visually and functionally."[10]

Some are trying new methods and markets, most are adding off-farm jobs as well as shuttling children to centralized schools. For some the spirit is hope, for others it is worry and fatigue from hanging on against great odds. Finally, some stories are about beginnings, told by the new or the young or the "beginning farmers." Of those, many talk with enthusiasm about being part of a movement (whether industrialized or sustainable) to create new paths in agriculture.

What is common to all the stories is that families feel the tension and weight of a new moment—for better or for worse. They know that decisions now, whether technological, political, corporate, or personal, are adding up to determine the future. It is the future not only of farms and rural communities, but many would say of healthful or unhealthful food, the sustainability or the ruin of land, the control or the decentralization of food systems, and the dignity or the exploitation of farmers around the world.

All of these families value the farming way of life that keeps land and family life together. There are conflicts about the different ways of doing this, but all of the families feel they are part of the quilt, securing "agrarian culture." When they come together in faith, they *know* what keeps them there. It is connected with their sense of God, the land, their call to do God's work.

The Time to Choose

Despite the pervasive language of inevitability and progress, agricultural concentration is the result of human decisions—policy choices and technical practices—that others with a different vision can reverse. Studies show many farmers distancing themselves from the answers of agribusiness with a clear consensus among them that a farming system based on moderate-scale farms offers the greatest benefits to the surrounding rural economy and to society in general.

Speaking to the Practical Farmers of Iowa in Ames, John Ikerd, professor emeritus of Agricultural Economics at the University of Missouri, critiqued the industrialized model of agriculture as undesirable and past its time, and indicated the vital signs of the coming of what he called the New American Farm. "Thousands of farmers are finding ways to sustain a desirable quality of life for themselves to support their local communities while being good stewards of the land and the natural environment. They may carry the label of organic, low-input, alternative, bio-dynamic, holistic, permaculture, or no label at all, but they are all pursuing common economic, ecological and social goals." He observes: "By their actions, these farmers are defining a new kind of American farm....The new American farm relies on the advantages of diversity, individuality, and decentralized networks of interdependent decision-makers."[11]

The "network of interdependent decision-makers" includes a growing number of non-farmers, urban connections of consumers, believers, and advocates. Many family farmers, new farm families, and local communities are conscientiously making alternative choices, stepping out of the corporate model, and creating alternative systems. There is a sense of a larger "we" that holds values, health, and heart over the bottom line.

Coalitions of farmers, churches, environmentalists, and citizen-action groups work on specific issues (rules limiting permits for large confinement operations, labeling food's source of origin, mandatory price reporting, etc.) to soften the effects or hinder the expansion of the corporate system while they hope to change it altogether. Subsidies to farmers, they know, benefit the mega-companies by allowing them to pay farmers less, and in turn they can use the grain to force farmers around the world to sell theirs to them even cheaper. Activism has gone to the top, protesting the power of the World Trade Organization that can dictate and even sue countries that do not follow their free trade laws. Farmers have left their fields for demonstrations in the streets of Seattle, Cancun, and Miami to join the world's farmers in protest. Together, in many languages, they unite as "campesinos" (peasants of the land) to speak for justice. "Until governments begin to value people more than corporate profit," wrote Wisconsin farmer and activist James Goodman, "the protests will continue, the struggle will survive."[12]

Pastoral Responses

1. Prayer of Thanksgiving
   God of all creation, we thank you for the inheritance our parents and grandparents have left to us. Show us the way that we might fully use these gifts wisely in order that the legacy we leave to our children may be acceptable in your sight. Amen.

   Let us consider our world
   Not as inherited from our parents
   But as borrowed from our children.

2. It is important to get around to visit farm families and to encourage storytelling around the kitchen table, over the fence, in the barn. Choose times when there is less farmwork pressure. If you stop by often and for short visits they will be less likely to stand on ceremony. Support them as they face difficult choices.

3. Church presence is noticed and appreciated for events like field days, fairs, farm meetings, local issue demonstrations. These are occasions to listen and learn, to understand what is valued and what is at stake. There may be times when you are invited to speak or feel you must make your position known from a faith perspective.

4. As a parish council or social concerns group, consider the following summary list as you set goals; use it as a reference point in doing the traditional functions of the church in relation to rural stress:

   - Attend to local values, beliefs, and attitudes, honoring tradition while also shaping new ways that help with coping with change.
   - Provide an economic safety net and a way of giving help that protects the pride and privacy of the family.
   - Provide emotional support and skills for those in transitional or tough times.
   - Support community development initiatives. Church people can be visionaries, advocates, and catalysts for community organizing and ethical development.
   - Nurture the faith experience of people, being sure in planning and scheduling that church events are accessible to all.
   - Speak out on important public policies using sermons, newsletters, newspaper columns to highlight issues related to justice and stewardship.[13]

5. Prepare a "Family, Faith, and Farm" program, perhaps after Sunday worship, and include a meal. Invite a speaker to keynote the theme, but work with three or four individuals or couples to reflect on the theme in relation to their own experience. They will be responders or part of a panel. It will give them the opportunity to clarify and articulate the values and commitments in their lives, and will be examples that encourage sharing by the participants in small groups. Suggested themes might be "intergenerational farming," "transitions," "improvements made for the land and water," "neighboring," "making do," "family traditions," "faith and hope."

6. In a world that constantly puts forth goals in terms of efficiency, competition, and profit, we must work to keep

our souls and spiritual language alive. Richard Cartwright Austin, pastor, farmer, and theologian, asks, "What did God know about farming" (in the face of the world's ways)? He goes through those seemingly unrealistic suggestions of the Bible: return land to original owners every fifty years [jubilee]; rest instead of compulsively working [Sabbath]; don't overwork the land or animals, don't chop down trees of the enemy; leave grain in the fields for the poor. What were these laws all about? "Community," says Austin. "It is about depending on and enjoying neighbors, keeping the whole living system healthy and fruitful generation unto generation."[14]

7. Study together *A Social Statement of Economic Life: Sufficient Sustainable Livelihood for All,* church-wide statement of the Evangelical Lutheran Church of America, 1999. Consider the key words: "for all"—the scope of God's concern; "livelihood"—the means by which life is sustained; "sufficiency"—what is needed; "sustainable"—a long-term perspective. These are often in tension with one another. "We must often choose among competing claims, conscious of our incomplete knowledge, of the sin that clouds all human judgments and actions, *and* of the graces and forgiveness of God."[15] For Lutheran rural resources, contact Sandra LeBlanc: *www.elca.org/do/ruralministry.*

8. A suggestion: At any rural event or church assembly, put out a roll of paper titled "One Hundred Ways to Save the Family Farm" and invite signed suggestions. It is a good awareness-builder at the event and provides good material for newsletters or bulletins. Below are a few examples from a scroll put out at a Dairy Expo and a CCLP Rural Life Gathering. Around campaign times we selected some of these suggestions and called them "Citizen Tips." The signatures have been omitted, but they represent thought from four states and a variety of people, both rural and urban:

- Write your people in Congress to strengthen the antitrust laws to guarantee a free market for the producer.
- Separate big money/corporations from government.
- We need to educate the public because most people from the cities don't realize what is happening to the small family farms and they need to know.
- Keep asking hard questions whenever someone asserts the inevitability of industrialism. Remind them that the economy should serve us. Remind them that life extends beyond the convenient and self-serving.
- Elect persons sympathetic to small farms issues.
- Believe in your own ability to make a difference.

9. Send some of your members (expenses paid) to church-sponsored rural conferences. Have them pick up materials to share and report on what they learned. They will bring your congregation's concern and support to the conference, and they will return expanded and renewed for the work ahead.

Pastoral work in rural communities, if sensitive to the depth of commitment of these families to their faith, the land, their communities, and the world, will respond by giving support. Offer a discerning and ready heart for what families may seek in this important and perhaps critical time.

CHAPTER 5

ALTERNATIVE MOVEMENTS

Story: "From the Pastor's Desk"

I have feasted at many tables in these summer months. Tables of love, justice, and hope; kitchen tables, conference tables, discussion tables, study tables, Happy Joe's tables, tables of my friends and family, and God's table.

At the end of June, I attended the Churches' Center for Land and People conference at Sinsinawa. The conference was titled "Come to the Table." Those gathered at the tables of this conference were a wonderfully diverse group of farmers, social workers, activists, clergy, and politicians.

We did what we often do when gathered at a table. We ate, shared, laughed and sometimes cried together. We discussed our food, the prices paid to farmers for food, and the values we as consumers support when we buy food. We shared recipes of alternative ways producers and even church communities can market foods. Through it all we feasted on hope. It was the best of table gatherings.

Gathering at tables, eating, laughing, and sharing food together is the way our community connections are strengthened. But what happens to the strength of our connections when a small number of corporations hold the power over the production and sale of our food? What happens to the health of our communities, our environment, our food, and even our own spirit when the corporations assign these things value based solely on their economic profitability?

Then the alternative values, spread for us at God's table, become more and more important. The food that we share is the body and lifeblood of Christ building us into community—freely accessible and open to all. Each person is given high value at this table. We need each of you at our table as we become the body of Christ. Won't you join us? *Rev. Sherrie Lowly.*[1]

Vision and Commitment

When food systems of the world are forged by a few powerful corporations with seed-to-shelf control, they are anything but local. Heartland fields are turned into rows and rows of corn and soybeans for animal feed and export while food we eat, grown in the United States, travels an average of 500 to 1,500 miles to our plates, not to mention food imported from other countries.[2] A study in 2001 revealed that farmers in southeast Minnesota, for example, had sales of $866 million in 1997, but spent $947 million to produce those commodities. Meanwhile, the 303,256 residents of the region spent $506 million annually buying food, most of which came from outside Minnesota, according to the analysis.[3]

Those involved in *alternative* agriculture and gardening feel the danger of industrialized agricultural practices that overuse land and animals, kill the life of the soil by chemicals, reduce farmers to contract workers, and put in question the healthfulness of the food. Individuals and groups committed to sustainability and community are creating new links that are local, land-friendly, and communal. To them it is a matter of stewardship, health, and justice. It is also a matter of spirit. Steeped in faith and spiritual respect for the earth's soils and growing things, they consider nurture of the land their vocation and contribution. They work reverently with the systems of nature to enhance the life systems. They work to build an economy on interpersonal relationships, local connections, and bioregional community. Their vision and commitment invite participation. They call our society to gratitude for earth and responsible preservation of its integrity for now and the future. It is an ethical and spiritual movement. Family farmer and direct marketer Janet Kassel says, "I garden for my soul."[4]

Gary Guthrie garden-farms in mid-Iowa. He reflects on his gardening and the meaning of "Eucharist" using the framework given by spiritual writer Ronald Rolheiser: receive, give thanks, break, and share.[5] Every spring as Gary prepares the soil, plants the seeds, receives the rain, he knows that farming is one of the few occupations that depend upon the forces of nature to make a living. Life is a gift *received.* As he sells his produce he gets immediate feedback: "My daughter asks for your carrots and she never asked for carrots before!" He needs their support, emotional and financial, as they need him for healthy food and a connection to the earth. This interdependence is reason to *give thanks.* The work is demanding and can be all-consuming. He needs to get away to coach his son's baseball team as a healthy discipline, as well as a way of connecting with the broader community. It is a recognition of human limits. He needs a *break.* Finally, whenever he visits a farmer friend in Bolivia or El Salvador he experiences the Eucharist. It is very humbling for a rich North American to be given the little food they have. It is *shared.* When Gary listened to the farming people there, he put their inspiration into a poem he titled "The Spirit of the Farmer." It ends (translated from Spanish):

> If you have thirst for life
> Come to the well of the farmer and drink from his life.
> When you drink water of this life
> Your life will never be empty.

A growing number of consumers in these alternative systems, both rural and urban seeking healthful food, are partnering. They too bring spiritual understanding. They know that food not only feeds the body, but in the receiving, sharing, and eating of it, the spirit is nourished as well. "People don't come all the way out here to get cheap food," says a Missouri farmer. "They come because it's fun and the berries are absolutely delicious."[6]

Seasons Affecting Alternatives

For all people there are seasons of planting and abundance, seasons of weeds and bugs, seasons of rain and snow, and seasons of drought. For alternative farmers and gardeners there are also seasons of thanks and communion, seasons of temptation and discouragement.

It is not easy to learn the ways and intricacies of the interconnected life systems of soil, water, climates, and habitats. It takes years of hard work, observation, trial and error, patience and commitment. With generous spirit gardeners and farmers share what they have learned in newsletters, field days, workshops, and annual conferences. This is a new moment for biocommunity understanding, learning to live at one with the earth.

At the same time, the economic world is in a season of speed and efficiency, of competitive business-dominated goals. Research projects at land-grant universities with government funds plus grants from corporations are largely focused on short-term, high-production, corporate-expedience goals (e.g., tomatoes engineered not for nutrition or taste but for long-distance travel). Their studies advance industrialized methods (chemicals, factory farming, bioengineering), and then try to find other technological ways to solve the very problems their methods have caused—overuse of soils, pest and weed resistance, concentrations of waste, pollution of water and air.

Farmers becoming technically proficient at one level find they must ask themselves whether they ought to do what agribusiness says is "necessary."[7] Must animals be confined? Must farmers buy huge machinery to bring in hay to feed them indoors when cows and cattle can be moved from field to field ("rotational grazing"), giving the grasses time to replenish before being visited again. This is not so much "alternative" as "natural," say Fay and Skip Stone. "We just had to be attentive and let Nature do her work. Our fields are richer, our way of life less stressful, and our financial outgo is less." They add reflectively, "Between our Catholic belief and our understanding of Native American Indian tradition, we can't help but feel that we farm the way the Creator intended, with care for the universe, and considering the future unto the seventh generation."[8]

For some this rejection of industrial ways came to them like a "conversion," a shock, almost like St. Paul being knocked off his horse. For Bill Welsh the catalyst was his cows gone mad and dying from hay contaminated by fertilizer bags. Bill and his son Greg became active advocates of organic farming.[9] For Rita Engelken it was the serious illness of all her children from her husband's spraying of chemicals before the dangers were known. She and her husband Ralph wrote a landmark book on *The Art of Natural Farming and Gardening* in 1981. Rita is well known for her beautiful and bountiful gardens and continues to teach her hard-won skills here and around the world.[10] For John Kinsman it was not only numbed legs, but his sons coming back from a Catholic college having learned about stewardship and justice.[11] This turned his farm politics totally around and he founded and continues to lead the Family Farm Defenders, is an officer of the National Family Farm Coalition, and speaks around the world in the international movement of farmers, *Via Campesino*. Each of these farmers made the slow, painstaking moves toward alternatives. Bill Welsh's son Greg pointed out that change means more than changes of practices; it involves inner change as well, and new relationships. "Transformations are never really instantaneous," Greg said, and explained that he went through a stage of becoming a "self-righteous environmentalist." He too had to learn Nature's ways of time. "In the end," he said with gratitude, "I am amazed at the life, love, and resilience in my father's heart, and to my surprise, in my own."[12]

Community

Those in sustainable agriculture, organic or permaculture gardening, and niche-marketing weather their seasons by joining others in supportive groups. They set up research projects of their own and share what they learn. They are developing production and marketing systems of increased breadth and sophistication. Producers, retailers, food preparers, and consumers are coming together to insure healthful food, fair prices, and awareness in the public sector. What is notable is that many of these communal efforts have the feel of faith-sharing communities where people share not only their learning, but their meaning, spirit, and commitment.

A popular series of gatherings of "alternative types" at the Churches' Center for Land and People was aptly named "The Called and Crazy." You qualified if you laughed when you heard the title because you recognized yourself in it. You had to come with your own story about when you were doing something those around you considered crazy, but you felt "called" to do. It was great fun but it also acknowledged the depth of spiritual sense of vocation. It let out the stress of being considered out-of-step with the prescribed world of competition and managed growth, and placed you among good-humored, supportive, faith-filled people open to a call.

There is energy in this rural and urban movement as people with similar seekings and values come together in new ways. In the Community Supported Agriculture (CSA) movement consumers provide capital as "shareholders" so gardeners have up-front money for seed and their labor. Consumers then receive weekly packages of fresh vegetables throughout the growing season. It is a true connection. Depending on the agreement, shareholder families may be invited to come and see, or occasionally to help with some of the work, a rare and special experience for many urban people. When a season is bad, consumers suffer the same losses as the gardeners. Many CSA families stuff the grocery bags not only with fresh produce but with recipes, nutritional information, words about the issues, or news notes about the CSA.

Educated consumers are also part of the movement as they begin to realize as they move through the grocery aisles that their food choices actually cast a vote for or against local and sustainable food production. In another movement, groups trying to resist exploitative trade situations around the world have added "fair trade" to the vocabulary of sustainable. They put Fair Trade labels on foods if the farm workers, usually in other countries, have been paid a fair wage. To operate outside the larger systems here and abroad takes great effort, and many consumers are willing to contribute by paying a little higher price to enable these efforts that more honestly reflect the cost of raising quality food and giving a just wage. Joining up in agriculture-related alternative efforts are also environmentalists concerned about soil, water, and air in our countrysides. Some join the resistance to factory farms, working along with farm organizations, citizen action groups, and churches to promote legislation that will strengthen regulations regarding the environmental impact of larger farms, as well as provide funding assistance to smaller farms for stewardship improvements. Meanwhile, advocates and services from the public sector are exploring the gifts and interconnectedness of bioregions, working with foresters, farmers, and land-trust organizations to preserve natural habitat and indigenous grasses.

What are backyards, poor neighborhoods, prison yards, and schools beginning to have in common? Gardens that engage, brighten, and heal. Gardening is a way of being and learning together, watching creation's miracle of growth, earning the fruits of hard labor, having something to give away. An article summarizing a workshop on turning a school garden into a school business ended their list of needed "steps" with "the Joy Factor."[13] This reminder is important in all alternative movements. With the stress of issues and demands of hard work, the danger is to tighten up in over-seriousness. It is hard to sell "health" or "just relationships" if the practitioners and advocates mostly seem overtired, too focused, or out there all alone against the world. Few people would want to join that. The spirit of God loves beauty, the spirit of God is mercy. The spirit of God is anti-grim. We thank God that the people we have met in these movements are in fact warmly spiritual and communities of joy.

Commitment and Prophetic Grace

For several years, until they outgrew the space, the Upper Midwest Organic Farming Conference[14] came to the conference center/farm/motherhouse of the Sinsinawa Dominican Sisters at Sinsinawa, Wisconsin. It was a natural fit: the shared love and respect for the land; the sense of space, rhythm, and beauty both outside and in; the careful preparation of organic foods; the style and warmth of community. Most of all, as they greeted each other in the halls and talked at the exhibits they recognized in each other, participants and sisters alike, their *committed lives*—the wholeness/holiness of life choices, work, and aspiration lived out each day for a better world.

People in traditional, industrial, and alternative farming alike know the importance of making farming possible for beginning farmers. Beginning Farmers programs are sponsored by a variety of interests. A number of sustainable and organic programs have been started by alternative organizations, and gardeners are glad to offer internships. The Churches' Center for

Land and People is forwarding a new collaborative venture to involve churches more directly in this movement and to include faith-based reflection as part of the program. Tony Ends, CCLP's Executive Director, has laid out a plan for this new "Partners in Stewardship Training": to recruit apprentice growers and give them experience, link urban and suburban churches with these apprentices, establish a new scholarship program, and return these trained young people to their own land and enterprises with customer relationships from urban and suburban church communities. Tony and his wife Dela have established a successful CSA operation and value-added enterprise, are active in regional alliance for farmer training, and have hosted interns at their own farm.[15]

The spirituality of people in alternative movements is a prophetic spirituality. It is the spirit of the God who said "I am making all things new." They are resisters to what theologian Walter Brueggemann called, in *Prophetic Imagination*, "the royal consciousness." Brueggemann described the psychic hold the Egyptian Pharaoh had over the Jews kept in slavery. And he says to us today: "We need to ask if our consciousness and imagination have been so assaulted and co-opted by the royal consciousness that we have been robbed of the courage or power to think an alternative thought."[16] The role of these new movements is to present a new alternative consciousness that can bring forth fresh forms of faithfulness.

This is a David-facing-Goliath confrontation between two very different systems. Agribusiness maintains strong lobbying every day in the halls of national and state departments of agriculture, presuming to "speak for farmers." They insist that bigness is the only way to be competitive, and technology the only way to be able to feed the world. They hire public relations firms to fill agricultural journals, public newspapers, and television with articles about progress against world hunger and ads assuring citizens that all is safe and environmentally sound. They discredit the massive street demonstrations against the control of the World Trade Organization, which has the power to undermine environmental and food-safety laws of nations in favor of global free trade.

In the face of this, individual farmers and alternative networks are doing the work of resistance and creative liberation. Against all the "expert" advice of the day, Joe and Rita Placke in southwestern Wisconsin broke from conventional farming and transitioned to organic. In three years they were selling milk to CROPP (the Coulee Region Organic Produce Pool, LaFarge, Wisconsin), a large organic cooperative that markets under the label of Organic Valley. Not only did they receive a better price but their soil was better and their cows healthier. "It's become common to say 'farming is a business,'" Rita said, "but...we look at things spiritually. We need to take care of what we have for future generations."[17] Alternative groups are increasingly successful: alerting the public to the dangers of food controlled in the hands of a few corporations; providing safe nutritious food; bringing back a sense of respect for the land as sacred and not to be violated; developing bonds of relationship both practical and spiritual between producers and consumers; and pressing forward environmental and food-safety regulations.

There are dangers in this success. Success has brought this small movement into the eye of corporate business. They can take advantage of the movement by appropriating and misusing their language, as in filling the media with misleading "green" ads. They can buy out smaller operations, lobby to alter government-regulated rules on the definition and regulations regarding "organic," and integrate the organic niche into their large globalizing systems. A different kind of danger is that some alternative ventures could themselves become more a business than a community enterprise and movement. They too can become so big that the temptation to "efficiency" takes over. The climate of pressure, on top of everyday hard work, can wear on both body and spirit.

Pastoral Response

1. Being part of an alternative (prophetic) consciousness energizes the community "to fresh forms of faithfulness and vitality," according to Walter Brueggemann. This is a critical call of our day. Our work for environmental

stewardship, fair prices, healthful relationships, and support of farming methods that assure a future for generations to come is a way we will participate in the transformation of our world.

2. Visit the farms and markets of alternative growers in your congregation and surrounding area. Bless and honor their work in planting and harvest seasons.

3. It can be a joy for churches to join in these creative movements. They have put to work the elements our religious traditions foster: earth stewardship, community, spirituality, and justice.

   - Church members are enlivened when they get to know and support local farmers and gardeners, or work a garden themselves.
   - Through partner-share programs and community-garden memberships, congregations can provide healthful food for their senior members and food pantries.

4. Suggest that your congregation become part of the Partners in Stewardship Training program of the Churches' Center for Land and People, a program for beginning farmers that will include faith-based reflection on stewardship *(cclp@mwci.net)*.

5. There are many ways to be involved and give support.

   - Seek out and get to know some groups in your region.
   - Show your support by attending events and buying produce.
   - Offer hospitality and church meeting rooms in a proactive way. It takes many meetings for area farmers and gardeners to develop the mission and logistics for working together. An open door, a welcoming space, a flip chart, and a pot of coffee go a long way to helping something happen.

- For church events, commit yourselves to buying locally (with fair prices) and be explicit in honoring the producers.
- Recognize your church members who are in the alternative movement by displaying their photos and brochures in a prominent place.
- Include prayers and blessings for every season in worship. Nurture in every way possible the deep spirituality of those committed to this work.

6. Social Concerns, Justice and Peace, or Rural Life committees should study the forces involved in present food systems and educate members to be more aware of choices they are making as consumers and citizens. Ask for denominational resources on food systems and alternatives. Here are two such examples:

    - An easy-to-use resource is the six cards prepared by the National Catholic Rural Life Conference called "Eating Is a Moral Act." The cards include: Eaters' Bill of Rights; Dignity of the Human Person I (farmer); The Web of Life Is One; Member's Creed; Dignity of the Human Person II (farmworkers); Water in the Web of Life *(www.nrlc.com)*.
    - A joint project of the Evangelical Lutheran Church of America and the Land Stewardship Project is the booklet *To Till It and Keep It: New Models for Congregational Involvement with the Land,* written by Dan Guenther, 1995 (1-800-NET-ELCA).

7. Send some members to the annual Upper Midwest Organic Farming Conference, currently held in LaCrosse, Wisconsin, in late winter. It is sponsored by the Midwest Organic and Sustainable Education Service, Inc. The gathering is large and spirited, the keynotes inspiring, and the workshops practical *(www.mosesorganic.org)*.

8. Know that if you want hope, if you want to know about and connect with good movements, contact at least one "alternative" group (a CSA, a farmers market, organizational newsletter or website, church-related rural conference). Talk with the people and ask questions. You will find that by tugging on one strand, you will be able to connect with a whole web of active relationships.

CHAPTER 6

GRASSROOTS ORGANIZATIONS

Rural Newsletter Headlines to Celebrate

"Victory: Pork Checkoff Ruled Unconstitutional," *National Family Farm Coalition*

"Farmers—Nation's True 'Survivors,'" *Wisconsin Farmers Union Network*

"Testing Our Character and Moving Forward Together," *Center for Rural Affairs*

"Building Communities: Finding and Mobilizing Community's Assets," *Institute for Policy Research*

"Making the Global Connection," *Family Farm Defenders*

"Writing New Chapters in the Local Food Story," *Leopold Letter*

"Citizens Deserve Big Thanks for Bottling Up Perrier," *Capital Times*

"Dialogue Sessions Gather Grassroots Feedback," *Illinois Stewardship Alliance*

"Taking Back the Food System: Healthy Farms, Food, Communities," *Community Food Security Coalition*

"Growing Community—and Vegetables Too," *Women, Food, and Agriculture Network*

"Victories for Family Farms, Environment," *Land Stewardship Project*

"Why Americans are Voting with Forks, Knives, and Wallets," *Organic View*

"Adding Values to Communities," *Cooperative Development Update*

"Recruitment Under Way for New Season of Learning, "*Michael Fields Agricultural Institute*

"Plenty to Celebrate at the Annual Meeting," *Practical Farmers of Iowa*

"Here's to Another Twenty Years," *Minnesota Project*[1]

Role and Contributions

Grassroots organizations are the heart muscles for rural cooperation, advocacy, and action. They are first-responders to critical issues and they are in for the long haul. They pressure for policies and they create newness with an eye to the common good.

Agriculture is at the cutting edge of the technological, bioethical, and global systems questions of today. Even the ruggedly independent must seek the help of others in personal decision-making about the way they farm and the kind of local and world community they want to build. There is a way in which grassroots organizations (whether local, national, or international, whether long-term or immediate, whether faith-based or issue-oriented) act as "base communities" for discernment, direction, and commitment.

Rural organizations demonstrate grace and hope in action. A collection of a single month's newsletters from grassroots groups of any heartland rural/small-town area with about a 150-mile radius would easily fill a file box. Read the headlines at the beginning of this chapter to know their spirit and influence. Imagination, prophetic resistance, and hope rise from those pages. And lots of names and faces.

The power of rural organizations is relationships. This communal commitment is counter to the habits of individualism fostered by large agribusiness that focuses on sworn-to-secrecy contracts and competition. Practical by nature, organizational members come together to get something done: better prices, protection of the community's water from a proposed factory farm, services for families that suffer from mounting stress, on-farm research for sustainable practices, influence on a new farm bill. But the glue for their cohesion and the groundwork for their action is rural-style relationships: person-to-person networking and membership-building; small-group huddles; potlucks and on-site field demonstrations; meetings that tolerate "side issues" and are moved by personal stories; humor, camaraderie, sharing of food; tractor pulls and carpooling.

Cultivating this sense of being-in-it-together is essential. In Richland Center, Wisconsin, seventh and eighth grade students of St. Mary's School took to the streets for a peaceful march and demonstration about milk prices. It was not a natural thing to happen. Despite the town's being in a rural area and dairy economy, few of the students were from farm families. But the principal and upper-grades religion teacher were, and they decided to teach the church's social justice teachings and principle of solidarity by having the students look at dairy issues. Townspeople signaled thumbs-up, and milk-price organizers from the area joined the march. One of those farmers, Ed Chitwood, said, "The issue is about families, widespread ownership, and a way of life that's being lost." He added, "It taught young people they could stand up for what is right."[2]

Nowhere else is interdependence so real and yet so challenging as on the land and in rural communities. All rural people live "downstream" from the land and water of others, whether polluted or kept healthy by those around them. All live "across the fence" from pollen drift that can, with one small wind, change their crops to uninvited genetic modification. In the late nineties New Melleray Abbey in eastern Iowa entered the fray supporting people protesting the plans for a large hog-confinement operation to be built near the monastery. Abbot Brendan Freeman said that monks aren't activists by nature but some things in life are worth fighting for. "Citizens around us have come to us and asked for help....This has forced me to look at what's really going on in agriculture." The people who gathered represented a spectrum of farm neighbors, urban supporters, rural and environmental interests, clergy and religious. "If you can organize third graders to get to the cafeteria," one of the sisters recalled hearing at a justice meeting, "you can organize a picket line." The monastery hosted the strategizing meetings facilitated by their own Director of Land Stewardship, Joe

Fitzgerald, and became the starting point for marches. Several weeks into it one of the monks stopped the abbot as he was on his way to a Rural Life Gathering to share the story of the protest. The monk asked him about engaging in civil disobedience. "He wanted to sit down in front of an earth remover," the abbot told the Gathering participants. "He's 75 years old."[3]

It takes long-term work and organization to develop common agricultural vision and practice in a watershed, on the bluffs, across open unprotected fields, on the edge of sprawling towns. Further, it takes rural/urban connection and vision to sustain both farms and towns. Family farm money spent locally circulates and multiplies within the community, whereas large-farm purchases of contracted supplies mean all the money goes out to corporate centers. For every five farms lost, a local business closes. Some organizations are particularly good at teaching community-organizing skills and coalition building needed for gathering and directing people's energies for leverage in issues. Congregations can join with organizations to add their gospel perspective and to witness precisely "as church."[4]

Many organizations have been building networks for years. They combine warmth and savvy. They know how to get support and are skilled in strategizing. From a strong center the work goes outward in reach and purpose. This demands a generous spirit. It is not easy and demands a lot of time. It involves the members in risk and presses them to grow. John Kinsman, president of the Family Farm Defenders, is active in the American Raw Milk Producers Pricing Association that brings dairy farmers together in efforts to name their prices. He knows what operating a farm plus grassroots organizing takes—long hours and unflagging spirit. Often John would say after another long evening of talk and signatures, "It was successful. One more farmer stood up and spoke for the first time." His eyes would shine. He was talking about dignity, the kind spoken of in church statements. To him, farmers standing up and speaking truth about their dedicated hard work and the system that was robbing them of their just reward was worth all the weariness and discouragement of the organizer.[5]

People in grassroots organizations are indeed heart muscles of rural life. They bring their insights, pain, spirituality, good will, and gifts to be put at the service of the organization's mission.

They have hope, vision, feel for the land, and a voice for justice. Despite their own pressures, these volunteers pour out their time and energies for the common good.

Seasons of the Organizational Heart

It is hard work to develop, direct, and maintain a project or organization. It requires good spirit to stay faithful and active in bad times as well as good. It is important to understand organizational seasons, what they offer and what they demand.

Organizations have the excitement of beginnings, like turning over the soil and planting in spring. Early leadership and a sense of urgent mission converge with purpose and passion. Yes, we want to create community-supported agriculture and we have the people who will make that happen. Yes, it is time to move with a spin-off from the parent organization and we have a director who can make it strong. Yes, the time is now to demand government accountability and our team is ready to organize a broad-based effort. The fields of endeavor are plotted and people gather to carry out the work.

Things grow, and the season of in-house structuring presents new challenges. More people, more time, and more money are needed to support this fullness and move forward on all the ideas. Conversations turn to concerns about accountability, communication, and coordination of efforts. How do we keep cohesion and personal spirit among growing numbers? How sustain energy in face of opposition or invisibility and the uphill nature of the work? How keep everyone involved? How weather a change in leadership? Long-term action is very demanding. Pressures both outer and inner make differences among members more noticeable. In a long-term organization, changes in the times and new issues require new approaches. Some things need to be let go of before new things can emerge. Organizations are also challenged to work together and go beyond their close-knit memberships. Robert Karp, executive director of the Practical Farmers of Iowa, calls it their *Pentecostal work*. "Sure, we can build consensus here, but how do we take that out into the wider world?"[6]

Yet despite all the challenges, grace abounds. In good times and hard, organizations celebrate their ongoing seedings and harvests, honoring their members and the fruits of their labor. It is both demanding and energizing to go to the annual gatherings. Exhibits show work accomplished. Positions and strategies are pounded out; members discern and install leadership; money is raised. At the same time, the gatherings have the flavor of reunions and festivals and prayer. No one would miss this time to be together. They feel the presence and power of their community, hear stories that touch the heart, rejoice in tales of victory, and renew their mission.

Increasingly women are not the invisible doers in the background, but are sought out or step forward as essential leaders in organizations. They are multitaskers, articulate, experts at community-building and communications in a network, and do not stand on ceremony when something needs to get done. Many women initiate action locally and have leadership positions in rural organizations.[7] Many have formed their own organizations to work on issues and to teach each other the farming skills they need as women in a male-dominated occupation.[8] At the Tri-State Fall Harvest Retreat for Women, Audrey Arner named their power and urged them to carry on "building strong base communities of celebration and resistance."[9] When women gather, they teach things they have learned, ritualize their unity, share their networking, strategize for actions around issues, and savor meals in common—the real food they have brought and prepared for all.

Grassroots organizations keep the heart-soil moist and loose so that new ideas can germinate. They stay close to the land where, as religious poet Gerard Manley Hopkins wrote, "There lives the dearest freshness deep down things."[10] In their meetings they touch Spirit in themselves, and in their hard-won unity go forward rededicated and refreshed. They know they must be strong-rooted like "perennials," returning year after year for the long haul. They do the spiritual work of developing root systems, nurturing relationships, and tending to sources of inner nourishment.

Sowing Goodness in Our Times

In the thirteenth century, amidst spiritual disputes, devastating poverty, and war, St. Francis of Assisi responded to the depression of his times. He named the seeds that people of spirit needed to sow in order to bring forth new life. The prayer of St. Francis is familiar to many: "Where there is doubt, let me sow faith; where there is despair, hope; where there is darkness, light...."

Likewise, the people in alternative movements and grassroots organizations work against the depression and oppression of our times. They do this in countercultural ways in the face of large forces that name reality in terms of individualism and corporate profit. They refuse to become numb and compliant. They "choose life"—in the soil and water, in interconnectedness of the land and people. "There are some beautiful things going on in the world," says John Kinsman, thinking of the resurgence of small dairy farms and co-ops in the Basque country of Spain and the efforts of farmers in India to protect their cultural heritage. "It's very inspiring to be around some of these people."

In our times, in the spirit of St. Francis, grassroots organizations work to sow newness for life:

Where there is fragmentation, they sow community.
Where there is apathy, commitment.
Where there is competition, cooperation.
Where there is opportunism, generosity and fairness.
Where there is depression, actions for hope.
Where there is powerlessness, work for justice.
Where there is destruction, care for land and people.
Where there is cynicism, trust in people together.
Where there is discouragement, strength in the Spirit.

Dis-Heartening Forces

At the same time, the organizations suffer the same dispiriting and disheartening forces of our times and need encouragement and support. While farmers organize for fair milk prices, the member base of their movement diminishes as farm after farm sells its dairy herd or loses the farm to exhaustion or bankruptcy. As farm, church, and environmental coalitions work for fair legislation and good land stewardship policies, agribusiness lobbyists flood national and state governments with imperatives of globalization. As urban and rural bonds for direct marketing enjoy widespread development, megamergers of food corporations and buyouts of new smaller ventures continue at a rapid pace. And as protests grow against unfair trade agreements forced upon developing nations, the corporate-government union gets stronger, and forces are mobilized against demonstrators in the name of national security.[11]

In this milieu of depletion, competition, and misused power, it is difficult for organizations to keep up their spirits and to avoid competition for limited resources, even among themselves. Beleaguered by wrongs and drawn into battle, they may feel little energy left to create the newness they envision. While they are working for others, who is supporting them? Who gives them energy to keep creating hope? How can we join them by keeping alive the language and practice of compassion, and common good, and justice? Even though a good number of our congregation members are in these organizations, do we as churches acknowledge and support the work they are doing for the health of society and for justice? Secondly, what are we doing as a congregation to join in these issues? "Our church has been fairly clear about our values and beliefs in relation to the land, the water, and toward democratic and decentralized ownership of land," says Anne Kanten, Minnesota farmer and advocate. "But our willingness to wade into the political battle necessary to put our beliefs into action has been less clear."[12]

Pastoral Response

As churches, communities, and individuals we owe much to these grassroots organizations that act for our good, and act (though we often do not notice) on our behalf. Many are members of our churches. The motivating spirit in the souls of most active people is faith, hope, love, respect for creation, commitment to the justice of the gospel, and a religious sense of community. Grassroots organizations put out into the world what churches teach, what baptism calls them to. The following are ways we can minister to their spirits and help them in their public missions:

1. Recognize their work as an organization; honor their members as generous contributors to society.

    - Express thanks by recognizing and blessing them in congregational settings of prayer and celebration.
    - Subscribe to their newsletters and respond to what they write.
    - Give personal and financial support.
    - As church representatives, attend their meetings, rallies, fund-raisers, celebrations.

2. Strengthen their spiritual connections.

    - Go back in this book to the section on "Prayers and Rituals for Sustaining Hearts." There is a Ceremony to Honor Rural Mission that invites participants to share their church, organizational, and institutional Mission Statements in the light of the Scriptures.
    - Listen well and mirror back to them their strengths.
    - Encourage them in the "ministry" they are doing in their organizations.
    - Provide a place for their area meetings.
    - Provide opportunities for their use of spiritual language.

3. Learn from grassroots organizations and spread their message.

    - Study the needs or issues they are addressing; speak about these in church and in other spheres of influence. Include them as agenda items to discuss in staff and committee meetings.
    - Incorporate concerns/issues awareness in sermons, conferences, writings, bulletins.

- Address in as many ways as you can the seeming shyness church people have with regard to claiming their roles as "organizers" or "activists."

4. Study the gospels. Notice that getting people in touch with their dignity and rights was important to Jesus' ministry. He questioned assumptions, took sides with the poor, and named "community" as the bottom line. As a result, he rankled those interested in keeping the systems tightly in place.

5. Raise to their consciousness the natural organizing skills in church people. They know how to build community and identity around values. They can name what is wrong. They watch and study, plan and build. They mobilize in time of need, and organize complex events. They have a thousand skills of integrating, getting things done, and working within intricate systems of people and land. Let them dare to be clear about their God-given powers and put them to the service of what must be done to make rural life possible and fruitful for all who participate in it.

    - If people are new to public demonstrating they can ease in. They will contribute their presence, which is always important in organizing, while they watch carefully how it is done. Mingle in the crowd and let them know you are there. Sign up for more information. The next time have a prep session for "sound bite" responses in case a reporter comes near. How would you articulate the issue, the purpose, or "why you are here" in one or two sentences? The third time, if there is an open-mike period, be ready to get up and speak. Tell them whom you are there to represent. Each time, bring more people with you.

6. Four definitions for the word *sustain* fit what organizations do for and with others. Churches have a special gift and call to help people in organizations with the third definition especially, and to make congregational decisions in line with the fourth:

to undergo without yielding
to support from below
to keep spirit from falling away
to give weight to decisions for long term.

7. Send for denominational materials for study on issues and principles. Consider together this challenge by Eva Jensen of the National Council of Churches of Christ (NCCC) at the church-sponsored "Come to the Table" conference:

    I believe, as churches, grassroots organizations, and people of faith who are concerned about land and people, we must bring to the table a voice that claims economic growth and profit are not the primary values on which we can create sustainable agriculture and rural communities....The economy is a human construct, a social creation governed by relations of rights and responsibilities between human beings, and maintained by social institutions. To be sustainable, economics must be firmly established in society and operate within the constraints of nature. Values that are informed by our faith and community-based perspectives include respect for human dignity and the integrity of creation, social and economic justice, a commitment to the common good, and a preferential option for the poor."[13]

8. The congregation itself is "organized" and has mini organizations within it. So take to heart this Number One of "Organizing": "Relax, and don't forget to have some fun! The issues at stake are serious, but if the work isn't fun at least some of the time, it'll be hard to recruit others to join—and you'll lose enthusiasm too."[14]

Chapter 7

LOCAL COMMUNITIES

Story

Then came the crucial question: And where are you as church?

We, a team from the Churches' Center for Land and People, asked this question as people of a rural congregation stood before a "map" on a wall of their church hall (large newsprint roll of paper) on which they had just depicted their "community." The drawing included representations of their homes, church, farms, schools, main street businesses, clubs, food pantry, local restaurant, quilting circles, bank, fire house, voting place, and other important but perhaps more distant places—nursing homes, recreational park, co-ops, grassroots rural organizations, county and state agencies, and shopping mall. By the time they finished, they had mapped out quite a large area, including several towns and main roads.

Each person, with a handful of smiley stickers, had come forward to mark places where they regularly interact with people in their community. The map filled up with color, smiling faces everywhere. Back in their places, they had gazed at the map with satisfied wonder: look how active and involved our handful of church people are!

In celebrating their life, they were ready for that question: And where are you as church? The silence that followed was like prayer as the question worked its way into every mind and heart. You could almost hear the "aha's" begin to rise as they studied the map and decided where to place the church symbols. Once again the map filled. This time they saw their life in the community and claimed it as church. *Miriam Brown,* OP [1]

Relationships, Interdependence

The soul of the rural community, town and country together, is communal. Interdependence, co-responsibility, and celebration are lived out—intimately and demandingly—on a day-to-day basis and for the long haul. Rural communities enjoy, depend on, and model fine-tuned interlacing of relationships: heritage and spirit, kin and new members, agriculture and small businesses, leaders and associations, youth and elders, café clusters and emergency volunteers, social wisdom and strong traditions of faith. Today's challenge of sustainability is felt personally, that is, with awareness that every gathering somehow relates to the health of the whole.

Missouri farmer Margot Ford McMillen had an eye for these interconnections as she described a gathering that was more than a gathering those hot August days of "working up" a bumper crop of tomatoes in the church basement. There were women, teenagers and children, townspeople and rural, core group and drop-ins, working and building bonds over their enjoyment of harvest, appreciation of food, and love of good company. She points out that they were in the church because "it was the one center left for our community" after homesteads and stores were plowed under by "production agriculture." But that day, "our canning ritual fights off the industry and brings a little of that community back....We neighbors have made a commitment to support small farmers and we're working it out in this kitchen." Young people come, she says, because they want to live in that kind of neighborhood and learn the skills others can pass on to them. "We're building new traditions on the old. Buying and trading with our neighbors creates a friendly time, lifting all our ships. So what's going on in the church basement...is a beginning of something new."[2] Relationships for sustainability. Heart-knowledge and bonding that make what community builders call "social capital": people holding together and creating viable futures.

From generations of living and working together, people's sensitivity and skills of interaction are well honed. They know the hopes of each other's lives and how things do or don't weave together. They know the contribution of each home, industry, service, and institution. Interchanges are the daily blood of the community and the workings for its future. All have a part in the commerce, spirit, and leadership that create the community's life and give a distinctive vision and personality to their "home."

Leadership and Community Commitment

Rural communities rely on the relationships built within and between associations, churches, schools, businesses, agricultural marketing, county services, and town hall. As members of one or more of these bodies—hired, appointed, or volunteer—people shape the social care of the community, integrating diversity, honoring contributors, and putting forth resources for those who are in need. They adjust and develop the economic interweavings of the community. They are catalysts for spirit, embracing hardships and celebrating accomplishments. At its best, this interaction among groups is unselfconscious and natural, the way things are done when community is small and talents are known and called upon.

People of faith are motivated and skilled for active involvement in their communities. In their churches they have the experience of making community with diverse members. They learn the acts of unity-building and celebration. They feel the work of community as a call and responsibility. Gospel traditions are deep in their bones—responsibility to be a good neighbor, offering self for the common good, sense of meaning and hope.

Personal leadership is fostered along the way. Statements like these are typical: "My wife and I had been working on the program committee for the festival for years, so when Richard Ingles was ill this year, they asked if we would co-chair it in his place and we said yes." "I've gotten to know a lot of parents and was active in school policy meetings. Some of them encouraged me when I thought about putting my name up for the board." As people gain experience they may work with other community groups in coordinating efforts for the "something larger." Communities are blessed when good leaders cluster and make things happen. They may or may not be elected, but they have learned to be inclusive and persuasive in building consensus and commitment for local efforts for community betterment and activities. The heart of rural community is relationship, and it is in these relationships that social grace is seen and celebrated in action.

Seasons of Celebration, Seasons of Change

People in rural communities celebrate the rhythms of holy events in intergenerational extended families—births, marriages, anniversaries, deaths. They nurture life and exchange ideas in everyday settings: at the local farmers' truck stop, around the quilting table, at ballgames, when dropping in on the shops and gathering places of Main Street. Special events are seasonal: town and church anniversaries, agricultural expositions, graduations, church bazaars, heritage days, school tournaments, and harvest festivals. Annual picnics and banquets honor those who volunteer: boards, services and outreach, fire and rescue squads, business and rural organizations. Faith-filled people participate in all these circles, enlivening them with generosity and hope. Their worship services and faith-sharing lift up the community intentions in prayer, and celebrate the action of God's grace in their midst.

But rural communities today are facing unprecedented and, in many cases, threatening change. Rural communities grew up and flourished as agriculture spread across the Midwest, populating the open spaces with farm families and providing centers for trade, church life, and social interaction. As rural life developed, towns took on their own distinct characters according to size and special attraction: ethnic culture, county seat, educational center, market hub, recreation or scenic attraction.

Two major factors have created a new picture for rural communities: the urbanization of American culture and the industrialization of agriculture. First, burgeoning interest of urban people for "land" and "country living" brings them into rural settings without understanding or appreciating rural rhythms, interests, and ways of relating. They come with urban ways: speed, mobility, less personal relationship with neighbors, shopping at national chains, and reliance on structures and policies to resolve conflicts or take care of the common good. Commercial sprawl is common to an urbanized life, but for rural people, strip-mall shopping centers not only threaten local stores but lack a sense of community and local identity. Traditional downtowns have served as meeting places and locus for community functions, so for rural communities, maintaining "Main Street" is a high priority. In less populated areas, where small towns and townships were once fairly self-sufficient, they now must think regionally for health services, education, social clusters, shopping, and even church services.

These seasons of change bring challenge to the ingenuity and spirit of rural communities. Hard economic times mean stress and limited time to devote to the common life. First, urban orientation draws youth and talent away to the cities. National stores with low-wage jobs have little tie to the community while displacing local businesses that have historically been generous in supporting community betterment and participating in the town's visioning. Second, as agriculture has become an "industry" and the production, processing, and marketing of grains and meats are consolidated by globalizing corporations, family farming has become less honored as a way of life and vital part of the community. It is being subsumed into a system of business that transfers money, people, and decision-making out of the local community. An ironic and devastating sign of the times is an empty meat-packing plant, once locally owned and providing good jobs, now threatened to be torn down and the space used for a Wal-Mart store.

In some rural townships a sign of the times is the arrival of corporate power to control local decisions. On October 6, 2003, about 180 outsiders, "a virtual who's who of factory farming," converged in Minnesota's rural Dodge County for a meeting of Ripley Township, a township with 109 registered voters. The issue was the placement of a 3,000-cow mega-farm in the community whose vast majority adamantly opposed it. Who were these visitors? Representatives, according to the sign-in sheet, of Land O'Lakes, Cargill, Ag Star Financial Services, Minnesota Soybean Association, Minnesota Soybean Research and Promotion Council, and no less than five Monsanto representatives, including one all the way from their corporate headquarters in St. Louis, Missouri (main supplier of rBGH, a genetically modified growth hormone used by big dairies to boost milk production). "This display by agribusiness and factory farm proponents," wrote a Policy Program organizer of the Land Stewardship Project, "is a clear indication of how local control is a problem for industrial ag."[3]

Upheaval and threat in this agricultural base means for rural communities losses of strong contributing families, local economic interchange, and the farm ethic of hard work and service. As farmers, workers, and small businesses work harder for less and less, they have little time or monetary resources to give to churches and local involvement, and in some cases become the people in need. Agricultural consolidation bypasses local suppliers, services, and processing enterprises. Farm-related money that used to circulate many times in the community now moves directly out to corporate centers. Additionally, as processing plants consolidate, mechanize, and "de-skill" jobs, people of other cultures are drawn in for low-paying jobs, suddenly diversifying the community's population and calling for new relationships and services.

A New Moment in Rural Communities

Whether facing agricultural diminishment, land take-over, urbanization, or cultural diversity, rural communities face questions of identity and spirit. The challenge of sustainability—social, economic, environmental, spiritual—is placed before them. Now more than ever there is a call to participate not only in healing, but in creating vision and spirit. What will sustain the hearts of the people in this changing time? How will they, in the words of Scripture, "choose life"? How does the community, discouraged by systems and trends outside their control and fatigued by personal efforts to survive, hold together and cross over into renewed life?

An Extension Agent in a county-seat town of some size was working with community leaders on vision-making. He invited a church person to talk with them about "The Soul of Community Leadership." The speaker placed their local task and decisions within the framework of the world's challenges of sustainability, interdependence, dignity, hope, and justice. "It is a critical moment," she said. "As leaders you are called to engage the journey as you structure relationships for the future. Around your planning tables you must consider the hearts and souls of your people. Given the direction of society for progress regardless of cost, the widespread disconnectedness from the land, and the challenge of engaging people to work for the common good, leaders like you have the unique responsibility/opportunity/call to frame your questions and make whole-community plans in terms of wisdom—soul."[4]

These are deep spiritual challenges in this seemingly "dark night" in the community. It is a time of great complexity. People of faith may identify this experience as a time of "exile." Some will hear it as a call to begin again. It takes great souls to recommit to one another, as the people of the Exodus did, moving through the desert to the river's edge where they "paused" before the unknown land before them. What deep commitments will be needed for today's rural communities to cross over and create new places of promise?

People will do the work of renewal in their own ways. It is not about a great leader coming in from the outside to take on a single issue, or about risking all for the cause. Rural community members work on what they are in—their groups, organizations, businesses, government—looking for ways to adjust for new times and coordinate with others toward new goals. Grassroots newsletters are filled with creative new ventures combining the talents of once separate entities. Always and foremost they maintain family, work, outreach, church, and public life, nurturing change within these areas. They bring this personal experience into the work of the whole. Individuals who take on their own growth challenges are able to understand and invest in the welfare of others.

Redemptive Gathering

The work of God is always with a "people," moving them in their journey together. Jesus in his ministry "gathered the scattered," and the gathering itself was redemptive. He was a man of his times, healing what needed healing, challenging what should be challenged, forgiving, celebrating, multiplying. Churches offer that spirit in these times to rural communities—healing, challenging, reconciling, celebrating, and most of all multiplying—multiplying the power of the goodness and the strengths that are there, helping people act from their abundance.

At a very deep level, churches foster in members the understanding that they are in community together. Through the practices of worship and song, history and heritage, picnics and fund-raisers, outreach and social action, churches develop in members a way of being "neighbor" to one another and to the world. These habits (virtues) of being neighbor hold up in hard times. It means people are ready to put forth extra effort to sustain spirit. Community organizing depends on the Spirit's "many gifts" that are offered for the good of all.

Pastoral and Spiritual Leadership

Pastors, lay associates, and congregation councils have a ministry of spiritual leadership that goes beyond the parish to the broader community.

1. Know your "parish," which in rural communities means the wide circle of town and country with its interacting groups and communal concerns.

    - Get around to the people and associations that give life to the community, represent the community's various voices, and give it its special flavor. In the rural way, sit down to chat, and return again. Hear the hopes, concerns, relationships, values.
    - Initiate and maintain intentional contact with community leaders and service providers. Create a notebook; fill in names and ongoing notes of conversations with: social services, Extension, health professionals, school faculty, religious leaders, business people, economic developers, agricultural professionals, mental health and medical professionals, city and county offices, elected officials.

2. Help church members see their work and life choices as faith-filled.

- Offer a community discovery process similar to the process described in the opening story of this chapter. Help your members see where they interact in the community, and have them consider where they are "as church." Help them expand their notion of Church to their relational and public life.
- Use bulletin boards and newsletters to display photos and describe actions of members active in the community.
- Say encouraging things directly to them: "Your leadership/volunteer work/job is a real ministry." "You have a strong and generous spirit in this community." "Your support of town celebrations blesses our lives together." "Your sensitivity to this issue (e.g., mall sprawl, farm prices, cultural diversity) speaks from the gospel of compassion and justice." People will begin to recognize that Grace is working in and through them.

3. Reflect the community in congregational prayer and ministerial reflection.

   - In Sunday worship remember special town occasions (graduations, festivals, openings of new community projects). Remember area intentions (new school year, weather-related needs, community decisions). Call people/groups forward to receive a special prayer of thanks or commissioning from the congregation.
   - Offer sermons and encourage faith-sharing around some of the biblical themes related to this chapter: being "neighbor"; pro-actively "choosing life" for the community; "gathering the scattered," leaving no one out; celebrating the Spirit's "many gifts" given for the good of all. Relate the mysteries of the Paschal season, (life, death, and resurrection) to the struggles of communities today. Preach forgiveness and compassion in ways that encourage responsibility and love for the whole. Place local challenges and opportunities within

the context of today's call to sustainability, interdependence, dignity, hope, and justice.

- In time of crisis (for example, a large factory shuts down, or several businesses move out of town), initiate and host a forum and invite staff of community agencies and services to be there to acquaint people with resources; work with groups in an ongoing way.

4. In parish councils and committees include discussion and reflection on community events and concerns on a regular basis. Ask: "What do we as people of faith have to offer by way of help or prophetic voice?" In ministerial associations and denominational clergy clusters, include community concerns in every agenda. Offer hospitality for community forums. In a planned way, send members of the congregation to conferences that put faith and timely concerns together so they can bring back new perspectives.

5. Facilitate a group process considering Jesus as model for roles in the community. A brainstorming process will evoke such roles as: Mediator, Healer, Agitator, Teacher, Spiritual Leader, Member, Gatherer, Reconciler, Friend, Liberator. Share back and forth gospel stories that illustrate these roles. Then in small groups have participants name congregation members who fulfill those roles in the church and community.[5] A variation of the process can help partnering or merging churches. After the brainstorming and the storytelling of Jesus' roles together, have each church group describe to the others who the people are in their churches that fulfill these roles. It is a good way for churches to get acquainted and begin to feel common bonds.

6. Study together the following graph, prepared by Cornelia Butler Flora, Director of the North Central Regional Center for Rural Development, that contrasts an older model Community Development based on needs, to a newer model Community Building based on strengths ("assets") that enhance participation and ownership.

Community Development	→	Community Building
Needs Assessment	→	Asset Mapping
Clients	→	Citizens
Individual Leadership	→	Community Capacity
Strategic Planning	→	Strategic Visioning
Deficiencies	→	Capacities
Dependency	→	Interdependency
Industrial Recruitment	→	Building from Within
Outside Evaluation	→	Internal Monitoring[6]

7. Be a catalyst for community-wide "assets mapping." Inspired by a day offered for rural church teams, dairy farmer Kathleen Vinehout returned to her small community and began organizing an evening session for churches, institutions, businesses, active citizens, and youth—a session for naming their assets and finding creative new ways to link them. In planning the event, she modeled the very thing she was highlighting—she went around and personally invited people and groups to cosponsor the evening. It was well attended, good-spirited, and generated a sense of community power.[7] Luther Snow facilitated the asset-mapping process. "Development," he said, "is creating a new link between two or more existing assets."[8]

8. "Will we dare to become the quilters of our day," asked keynoters of a rural conference, "to create a pattern still being revealed—moved by compassionate caring and hope, to establish a new order, a new arrangement of our reality?" Look in your communities, they said, for wounded healers; for those who are gifted in compassion and ability to unite people; for understanding, non-judgmental hearts; for prophets of new possibilities, willing to stick their necks out in proposing a pattern never tried; for people building bonds where others see boundaries.[9]

CHAPTER 8

INSTITUTIONS

Story

The business of forming the gentle land between two great rivers that we know as *Iowa* began when the glaciers moved north, some ten thousand years ago. This land played gentle host to its creatures. And the eagle swooped over the land and saw that all was good.

But while Iowa was going about the business of being formed, other business was underway in this place called the Fertile Crescent. Other groups were developing ways to tame the land so that it would produce their food. The business of agriculture was born. And eventually they found Iowa, and realized this was a land most suited to agriculture. The prairies succumbed to the plow, and swales to the tile. The gentle land shuddered under the clanging of steel and the weight of concrete. The land responded with its bounty, but there was a cost.

The unfinished business we call Iowa is now confronting the business we call agriculture and commerce and asking many questions. It is asking if the tools for agriculture provided by the land grant universities and by agricultural industries are adequate to protect and nurture this great land. It is asking if the people of Iowa can continue to count on its agriculture for clean air and water. It is asking who will live on the land. It is asking why agriculture more and more regards its peoples as laborers rather than as partners and lovers of the land. It is asking if the eagle has a future.

The Leopold Center for Sustainable Agriculture, located at Iowa State University, has helped ask many of these questions, and provided a few answers. For the last eleven years I have had the great opportunity and privilege to lead the Center on its quest. In a few short months I will step aside, but rest assured, while I have much unfinished business, the Leopold Center will always be a part of me. We must all work to protect the eagle. *Dennis R. Keeney* [1]

Contributions

Institutions can help sustain the land and the heart of rural families and communities. It is often difficult to think of state-related institutions as having heart. Largeness, politics, and bureaucratic red tape can mar the image and workings of the institution. Yet agencies, services, and educational institutions experienced on the area and local level are a notable part of the sustaining networks people depend on to research what is needed, update agricultural practices and small businesses, help communities in development, advise people in need, and provide programs that protect and enhance the land.

Institutions are made up of individual people, and many of those individuals have trained in educational and service professions because they desire to work for others. They want to bring their vision into the process and have the stomach to "work things out."

Wisconsin sustainable farmer Greg David won the election to become Jefferson County Supervisor. He was subsequently appointed to be a member of the University of Wisconsin Extension Education Committee. In that role he took the opportunity to speak to what he called "ethical and sustainable" programming, being concerned about the economic context of a market-driven, corporate philosophy of profit. When he asked this item to be put on the agenda at the next meeting, "discussion devolved to a question of, 'What is sustainability? And sustainable what? Economics? The environment?' Our committee needed to know what we were perceiving to be ethical about, before they could assess the ethical behaviors of the situation. Seemed reasonable." Greg e-mailed friends and organizations of the "civil society" to help him put together a Power Point presentation. Productive discussion ensued, involving other groups. "Awareness," he said, "is key to creative actions of resolutions."[2]

This engagement also illustrates what Cornelia Butler Flora of Iowa State University said is a strength of Cooperative Extension. It is at the intersection of the three spheres of society: market, state, and civil society. It can bring these groups together in appropriate ways to reconfirm visions and to determine action.[3] Look again at the opening story of this chapter. It also illustrates the dedicated good will of those willing to bring their vision to the table.

In the best-case scenario, individuals and institutions are united in their service of the common good, combining public resources and personal commitment for the present and future of families and communities. These leaders can provide a wide variety of supportive, educational, and empowering programs and do so with empathy and care. State-funded offices provide rural hotlines to respond to emergencies and chronic stress. They train volunteers who have been through hard times themselves to help people through financial and family crises. In a proactive way, institutions are also helping communities with "assets-mapping" to identify their strengths and to connect these assets in new ways that would create something new.

Seasons in Institutional Life

People within institutions, like everyone else, experience the warmth and cold of the seasons. Individually and as departments they have successes and failures, enriched and broken relationships, encouraging and conflicting processes. Political climate can change overnight through elections or appointments, or over a period of time as public opinion or needs shift in regard to policies, goals, and funding. As we have seen, there are pressures and conflicting viewpoints from the other two spheres of society—economic (business or "market") and civil (non-profit, citizen groups) regarding "the common good." The state sets regulations to insure stable conditions for the market, but also has responsibility for the public welfare.[4] All of these factors, personal and societal, impact internal cohesion, working relationships, sense of the mission, and chosen processes.

Public institutions should not be controlled by the money of the "market"—for example, through contributions to land grant universities for research directed to finding ways to minimize hog odor primarily for the purpose of reducing objection to factory farms. University of Missouri professor John Ikerd clarifies the role of those in public institutions: "As a scientist working in the public sector, working for the taxpayers, it is not my job to attempt to stop the industrialization of agriculture. However, as a public sector scientist, I do have a responsibility to question whether or not we should be using public dollars to 'promote' industrialization. Our job is to provide people with information. The people must decide whether they want to stop something or promote something based on that information."[5]

As a growing number of farmers are looking for ways to distinguish their products and create their own customer base, Richard Klemme, Associate Dean for Agriculture and Natural Sciences, University of Wisconsin-Madison, said Extension's work has shifted as well, "in order to meet the changing needs for education in the agricultural community." He commented, "This is a significant change for an extension organization that has a long and rich tradition in dealing with traditional farming and mainstream commodities, and a reputation for providing services for larger producers rather than small ones. We currently have several work groups addressing small farm issues, sustainable agriculture, and the new market/consumer-based business throughout the state."[6]

Locally, change in agricultural expectations, commodity marketing, and the need for business strength in a community may bring not only stress but also conflicts. A large institution providing a variety of programs might find itself in the middle of varying interests or local disputes. What seems good to one farmer, community leader, or business manager may seem wrong to another. In a small community what one decides to do directly impacts another. For example, a farmer goes to an educational institution for production and financial advice to expand the size of his beef operation to meet the family's needs and goals. A neighboring family may look at this institutional assistance as promoting "bigger is better" at the expense of their "small is enough" goals. At the same time that neighbor may be going to the same institution for assistance in cutting input costs and finding alternative markets in order to remain sustainably in business. That ethical concerns are part of the public sphere is clear as universities grapple with such questions as "Who Owns the Land?" in national conferences, and speak to the ethical dimensions of food systems at church conferences.[7]

There are town and country differences in concerns and goals as well. Town people may seek a consultant because they are concerned about endangered air and water for the community, while agribusiness farm organizations talk to consultants about how to attract larger farm operations to increase milk production or cattle-yard power in the state. At the same time town and country people alike may seek assistance in setting up local food systems that will connect rural and urban, farmers and consumers.

Institutional administrators need to keep up with the needs, balancing traditional and technological service for agriculture, and develop skills for issues tied to entrepreneurial farming approaches and urbanization. Klemme said they have moved from set programs to "self-directed teams," partnering agents with other government and campus agencies for range, added expertise, and staff resources.[8] Whatever the approach, institutional personnel, often in the middle of differing views, find themselves using their training in conflict resolution in everyday work in the community. They need not only heart but sensitivity and skill.

Successes and Challenges

Institutions can help build community around a program, issue, or need. An example of needs served by good people in institutions in the rural area over the past century is the 4-H and Youth Development cooperative programs across the country. They identify developmental goals and programs for boys and girls to grow into responsible and successful rural adults based on images of Head, Heart, Hands, and Health for the betterment of community, country, and world. Over the years this program has impacted attitudes and values of youth that in turn have successfully impacted behavior. Many land grant universities have beginning-farmer programs so that those entering agriculture, whether young or second-career, receive the help and support they need to get started in agriculturally complex times. A few of these are designed specifically for value-added and alternative methods.

Local groups can apply on the federal level for the USDA's Sustainable Agriculture Research and Education (SARE) program. One such group—The Research, Education, Action, and Policy on Food Group (REAP)—was able to launch its "Homegrown Lunch" project with classroom presentations to over 1,400 children in 20 elementary schools to appreciate good food and sustainable farming. Every effort for good use of public monies is important. Yet this was in the face of an outgoing governor's gift of state monies to the Farm Bureau to develop its own "Ag in the Classroom" curriculum with extra financial help and editorial oversight from the corporate giant Kraft Foods (Philip Morris).[9]

Within rural communities, institutions are asked to do more and more, often with less money and fewer personnel. "Farm stress does not only affect the farmer," says a dedicated agent, "but those who work with them as well." He has worked for several years with one farm family who have so little cash flow that they live on bread, peanut butter, and milk from their own bulk tank. "What can you do but pray?" he thinks seriously to himself. Then he goes to another farm and they seem to be flourishing. The disparity of incomes is enormous and causes stress throughout the neighborhood. At the same time, field specialists, service workers, and educators funded by various levels of government are being thinned and are doing twice the work. They must cut back programs and, like non-profits, have to seek hard-stretched grant monies to support their work.[10] Farmers not only want production information and assistance, but ask for help understanding the micro- and macroeconomic forces at play in the new business environment that can change in a matter of months. All decisions have an impact on rural communities, and many community participants realize that not all change is good. It is critical as positions are cut and programs streamlined that those influencing decisions are truly motivated by a vision of environmental stewardship and justice, and not overly influenced by the source of the funding, whether governmental or corporate.

The Struggle

The inspiring, challenging message of Dennis Keeney opened this chapter. He was about to retire (1999) as director of the Leopold Center for Sustainable Agriculture. The Center, established in 1987 and located at Iowa State University, funded research projects and educational events in nearly all of Iowa's ninety-nine counties. Frederick Kirschenmann, well-known farmer and theologian of the heartland, was so impressed with the Center's record of people participation on the local level that, despite reluctance to leave his successful farm in North Dakota, he decided to apply in the wide search for a new director. When he came for the interview he was struck by the number of scientists, mostly young, committed to doing research that would make farming more profitable for family farmers, less damaging to the environment, and more conducive to building strong rural communities—the same values to which he was committed. Chosen as director in 2000, he traveled all over the state and spoke with hundreds of Iowa farmers, urban and suburban dwellers, senior citizens, and students. The staff of the Center listened to community "conversations" and worked hard with the people to produce more value and retain that value on the farm while simultaneously restoring the natural resources on which all agriculture depends.

One year later the Center's budget was cut $250,000, and in May of 2002, the Iowa Legislature in a budget crunch transferred $1 million (86 percent of the Center's budget) out of the Groundwater Protection Fund that makes the Center's research possible.[11] The hardy Center vows to struggle on.

Pastoral Response

1. For the benefit of their members, it would be good for the pastor and congregational leaders to know the mission and resources of the local, county, and state agencies and institutions available to the people—services, programs, and expertise.

   - Arrange to meet directors and staff to share common concerns and learn how they might complement each other's work.

- Identify those with special empathy; give them the appreciation they deserve and the support they may need in view of the stress of their work and, perhaps, the bureaucracy within which they work.
- Call on the services of these skilled and committed people when appropriate; work with them rather than create parallel services.
- Showcase the agencies and services at church functions or provide collaborative programs for family life or community welfare. Many of the people in those services are in our churches and are looking for ways to work together.

2. As the opening reflection indicated, rural-related institutions have a challenging responsibility vis-a-vis large questions. How can we help our institutions be "adequate to protect and nurture this great land"? Do we as churches help to develop a vision? Do we take part in public discussion, whether in our own church halls or in institution-sponsored conferences? Land grant universities as a public trust must hear our voices as they grapple with how best to work on behalf of agricultural sustainability, stewardship of the earth, fair prices and market systems, with the common good and future generations always in the heart of the questions.

3. The church itself is an institution. It is one that many rural communities count on for stability and hospitality. It is a symbol of being there amidst change, diminishment, and redefinition.

   - Taking this as a call, congregations should look for ways to be open and inviting, reaching out and drawing people together.
   - In all its dealings with others it should be fair and compassionate. It should model what it preaches about respect for all and stewardship of resources.

- In times of questions or conflict the church can provide safe space, a forum for community discussion and discernment, and perhaps even healing. The church brings not only the gift of the prophetic, but the gift of reconciliation.

4. Active laity may hear a call to work more specifically in the institution of the church as an associate in ministry, lay minister, deacon, elder. Encourage this in your church. Those who have experience in the rural world will be good in ministry, and the special training will open theology skills for them, and a broader understanding of rural realities. One lay minister wrote in a reflection paper: "If I didn't have the Lay Ministry program I would have been looking through a keyhole and not seeing the whole picture. It was like opening the door."[12]

5. The church can take its role as an active voice in its sphere of "civil society." Today the power of the economic sphere is inappropriately dominant in its influence on the sphere of polity. In the case of the Leopold Center, agribusiness is the winner with funding for sustainable research virtually eliminated. In such a case the right people must hear a strong challenge from members of the church.

6. At the end of his Open Letter to Iowa promising that the staff of the Leopold Center would put all their energy into finding alternative support and also encouraging people to let their voices be heard, Fred Kirschenmann quotes the wisdom of Harold Morowitz applicable to all in the heartland: "Conformity is not necessarily a virtue, hard work is almost never a vice, optimism is a moral imperative, and a sense of humor helps." And Fred adds gallantly, "Don't ever give up."[13]

Chapter 9

YOUTH

Story

A reader e-mailed me a question a couple of weeks ago. The reader [of the author's Web site column] asked how I could keep up with helping Dad on the farm yet keep up with my homework and other school-related activities. Well, it is very hard to do.

I do not have specific chores that I have to do every day. Dad does all of the chores during the week and I help him out whenever I have time to do so. I stay busy during study halls at school, (use my time wisely) and I do a lot of homework after school or on weekends. I help Dad on Saturdays and do my homework and write my weekly journal on Sundays.

I usually watch only about an hour of television each day and that includes the news. I do not have that much free time. I do not have much time to play computer games or watch movies. We do not believe in working on Sundays, but sometimes we are forced to do some work, for example, sort and sell hogs for market.

I wake up at 6:30 each morning and go to bed about 10:00 each night. I often read for a short while before going to sleep. With my long, active days, I sleep well each night! I have more time to help on the farm when there is no school or during the summer. That's when I really help a lot with fieldwork, chores, and other yard work. I still manage to have time to do other activities like 4-H, FFA, band, and so on.

I wonder what life is like to live in a town or even a big city. I bet someone my age, living in town, has a lot different list of activities that he or she does in a day than I do.
James Frantzen (at age 13)[1]

Early Sense of Place and Seasons

For the adult, recapturing the heart of their youth involves a graced "remembering when." Their hearts and roots stay with them on their journeys throughout life. The farms they grew up on formed them, the impressions and images capturing them forever. As very young children they explored the great outdoors. The acreage seemed like the whole world. Mommy and Daddy own all this? The vital connections unfolded. Down the road a piece were the neighbors, a little farther the church, school, town—all part of their life as members of a vibrant community.

They learned that "to everything there is a season": times of work that to them seemed fun; times of sorrow, like the serious injury or death of a close friend or neighbor (farming is one of the most dangerous occupations in America); times of change, from winter into spring and summer into fall, with machinery to match every season; times to wonder how a little seed grew into a giant stalk of corn; times of visiting and making big gallons of lemonade; times of new birth, with the cows licking baby calves clean; times of being given new roles and responsibilities. When you talk to farmers today, these are the experiences that formed them and what they are trying to pass on to their children.

Such a process does go on in the young today, even though times are changing. Rural teens have natural daily ways that help them develop belonging, mastery, independence, generosity, and faith. With care, despite complex schedules, off-farm jobs, distant urban schools, their parents can help them stay connected, involved in the home and farm, part of a wide relationship. They will learn mastery when taught just enough and left to work out their patterns themselves, as well as learn how to deal with frustration. They will grow in independent thinking if allowed a part in setting rules and planning. And they will learn generosity as they see it modeled and when parents help them learn sensitivity and how to work well with others.[2] The faith life of teens is often hard to detect. Yet they absorb much from the family's prayers and traditions. Thus they grow in place, knowing what it means to belong, to be of and from "here." They grow in the spirit of the land and the profession and vocation of farming—with an experience of God in the midst of everything.

"Remembering when" also includes times when life's seasons didn't seem to balance right or fairly. Seeing adults make tough decisions on finances, needing to go without, dealing with why a disease took the life of a favorite cow—these experiences press youth to early maturity and strength. Many would say as adults that God's spirit was demanding a place in their hearts especially in the worst of times. They realized their dependence on God and prayer and the importance of a larger church community to help carry the burden. In it all, very few grew up without saying, "Thank God I'm a country kid."

Contributing Roles of Youth

Youth from farms offer great qualities to their peers and the larger community. They are grounded and work hard. They know the give and take of working out family chores and relationships of kin. They have learned to take on responsibilities and think for themselves in daily work and emergencies. They have a sense of managing time as illustrated in the opening story. They balance the demands of home, farm, school, church, community.

Just as a pastor might conversationally ask parents about their social and organizational connections in the area, the same question addressed to the rural youth of country and town alike will likely evoke an astonishing list of interactions and activities. Besides sports and extracurricular activities connected with the schools, many teens belong to 4-H, FFA (Future Farmers of America), or youth programs of farm, church, or civic organizations. "Belonging to" means hands-on projects, learning practical skills and responsibilities, taking positions of leadership in their councils, and participating in state and even national meetings. As they develop they often become coaches and mentors for younger members. At church they are initiated into service and outreach, take positions in Sunday worship, participate in religion classes, and once again, help with the children. Young people are very visible as helpers in parish events and festivals, and carry over that spirit to activities of the community at large. If offered responsibility, they can put together their own tents or displays, run games, provide entertainment, or present demonstrations of some new techniques and processes they are learning.

It is an expectation in small communities that everyone contribute, and rural youth learn to give to the whole at a very early age. When asked about their roles in the community, young people of the Wisconsin Farmers Union (WFU) from farms and small towns answered in recurring themes: "I help out...participate...volunteer...provide information...listen... voice my opinion...work on the farm...learn the issues...represent...bring up new ideas." As others of them said:

> *It is very important to be involved in farms, the community, organizations, and churches, to learn more, help others, and let my voice be heard.*
>
> *Growing up on a small beef/crop farm I have learned a lot about the importance of agriculture and its role in our national economy and in all our lives. It is important for youth to gain an understanding of farming and production agriculture even if they don't farm later in life. A strong community understanding and support is essential to ensure a strong future for American agriculture.*
>
> *In our community it is hard to get youth involved because many grown-ups think we can't handle the responsibility. I belong to the Cadott FFA Chapter where I am the president, and to the American Legion Junior Auxiliary where I am vice president. I was also confirmed at St. Rose of Lima in Cadott.*[3]

Coming of Age, Growing Pains

Seeing such evidence of the contributions of youth, we might need to step back and reflect. Are they doing so much that we miss the fact they are still growing, are subject to the usual teenage growing pains and anxieties, need our praise, guidance, security, and affection? Think in terms of numbers alone. There are fewer and fewer "kids from the farm." Classes in agriculture need to shift to urban interests if they are to fill classes. Numbers in Future Farmers of America have dropped dramatically: reduced farm population; overall reduction in high school numbers; recessional farm economy that affects attitudes of production farmers and administrative decisions; drastically reduced funds for vocational ag teachers; zero growth potential for production agriculture with few opportunities for new farmers.[4] Where is the young person's dream to stay in farming, given this somber future and their observation of the stress at home?

Youth today live in a complex world of many scenes and influences. Consolidated schools and the media expose them to urban styles, pace, and values. In normal teenage rebellion their rural lives may become distasteful to them. Their farms or small towns can begin to seem too small or unimportant next to bigger city life or the Internet's global connections. Natural teenage loneliness and alienation can spoil their sense of connectedness, intensified because some of their friends have no idea what farming is. With family life stressed, parents working off-farm, and friends and kin moving away as their farms close, teens can feel ignored and adrift. A pastor knew about the consistently falling prices but few parishioners talked to her about farm-related problems. But she noticed more irritability among the young people she was working with in the Confirmation classes. "If I pull them aside," she said, "they will talk about working harder on the farm, or that there's more friction in the barn. Others will say their mother's working off the farm now, so they have more to do in the house, watching the younger children or cooking. If you watch the kids, you will see their behavior change when something's going on at home."[5] In these conditions they may seek comfort with alcohol and drugs. They are more prey to peer pressure and unable to find adult connections that support them.

Expressions about themselves in regard to these challenges are tentative: "I try...you can't do everything...making your way...forced to be perfect...avoiding drugs...trying to fit in...fear." As young people graduate and move away to college or work, it is more difficult for those remaining to socialize and to network effectively or to form new ventures. One young man had to search out someone considerably older to start up a small gardening and marketing cooperative.

Expanding the Mentoring Circle

It takes a village. And so the church can be a catalyst to encourage school and community initiatives that support youth proactively. Some schools, besides taking a critical look at the side effects of their accent on sports, help bond students with their communities by building into the curriculum projects that link them with the knowledge and wisdom of their farmers, leaders, innovators, and service-oriented professionals. Some demonstrate experiences of entrepreneurship so students can see how they can succeed in their local community.

In a process similar to assets-mapping, individuals, organizations, and institutions can put their heads together to see what they have to build on in relation to youth to provide positive help. Neighbors can now and then invite youth to their homes or farms to enjoy a new setting, to try a new cookie recipe, play basketball, even rake out the barn (one mother said young people like work that is real, not made up; helping on a farm they know is real). Foundations and businesses can be sure some of their funds go to youth development. Congregations can open their doors for after-school or evening activities.

Churches are very good at helping in the areas youth need: to belong; to feel capable and experience success; to be independent and be able to influence; to be generous; to feel meaning and purpose in their lives. Scriptures and careful teaching can bring these needs and values together in helping youth integrate their personal growth and faith life.

Youth live in a noisy world, yet thirst for quiet. Busyness is the life all around them. Do more, see more, learn more, practice more. The over-commitment of time by rural youth is at issue in competing for their hearts and minds. Yes, youth need to build skills and character in themselves that often come through these activities. But team sports can be all-consuming and affect the whole family. It takes discernment for a congregation or ministerial association to know when to join the youth where they are, and when to provide alternative activities.

Young people today are alert to community issues. Again, churches can give opportunities to take part in widening circles of concern, to express their passion for justice. Seventh- and eighth-grade students made signs and marched after studying the plight of farmers and the Christian imperative of solidarity with the poor and dispossessed. Though only a few students actually lived on farms, all began to see how important this issue was to the whole community and responded. Their placards read "Got Milk. Got Price?" "Peace and Justice for All." Teachers, parents, and area farmers affiliated with the American Raw Milk Producers Pricing Association (ARMPPA) were proud to join them in this effort to raise awareness of just prices for family farms.[6] High school students can attend rural meetings both in the youth programs and with the adults. Most farm organizations have programs for youth and many parents encourage their teenagers to participate in the meetings, prepare exhibits, show animals, and attend rallies. Youth invited to be part of adult panels are appreciated and it is an expanding experience. If they are given something to do, youth respond.

Finally, what the young people want of the adults in their lives is: "Be there and listen; stress how much you are there for us; know when to step in and when not to; give us inspiring words; challenge us with responsibility; give credit where it's due; help us with our real problems...."

Pastoral Response

Youth need empowerment and the perception that adults in the church value them and give them real and useful roles in the church community. Don't just ask them to *join* a choir, ask them to *form* a choir. The church can assist the youth with creative activities in music, theater, arts, or other possibilities as a means of ministry within the church. Youth are able to lead tasks, mentor the faith of those who are younger, assist and attend Bible camps or retreats, raise funds with generosity. The church can assist their young people with positive risk-taking and positive peer relationships to build self-esteem and make healthy decisions.

1. Create communities of faith that nurture the following "assets" in relation to developing strong youth, using asset (not deficit) language:

- Focus on children and adolescents (not "troubled youth")
- Intergenerational community (not age segregation)
- Shared responsibility (not self-interest)
- Approach: expand asset-building actions (not buy new programs)
- Unified (not fragmented) vision
- Connected socializing systems and consistent (not conflicting) messages
- Focus on intentional redundancy (not efficiency) in asset-building experiences for youth
- Youth as actors in the process of change (not objects of programs)
- Long-term commitment (not constant switching of priorities)
- Engaged public (not civic disengagement)[7]

2. Youth, in their thirst for real spiritual experiences, are not so much interested in straight Scripture or "theology." They are active and want to feel things personally. Popular music and storytelling can give meaning and evoke spiritual understanding. Rote prayer may seem less meaningful than meditative, intuitive, and imaging prayer. Involvement of hands-on serving of others, coupled with meditative prayer, may reach youth in a way that repetitive liturgy perhaps doesn't at this stage of their lives.

3. What will speak to the youth of today?

   - Why aren't today's youth in church? Has faith development become more optional? Are faith and life disconnected? Pastoral response to the heart of youth may bring into question these issues. Yet youth can be very responsive if we catch their hearts. They want more than an intellectual approach to religion—something more spiritually intense, what some would call an authentic experience of God.

- Remember, said one educator, that in the developmental stages of adolescents these are the "wonder years," the years for questions, and the years for awesome discoveries. Remember, too, that the searching does not end in adolescence. Adults can help young people by admitting they do not have all the answers and by themselves being willing searchers.[8] Be sure to notice, however, that some youth have very special spiritual sensitivities. Do we nurture these gifts as much as we might nourish, for example, a special talent in music or art?

4. Consider the online course "Rural Youth Ministry" offered by the Center for Theology and Land, Dubuque, Iowa. It is designed to explore practices that help involve young people in the life and ministry of their rural and smaller membership congregations. Website: *www.ruralministry.com*. E-mail: *ruralmin@wartburgseminary.edu*.

5. Honor your youth and pray for them on their special occasions, such as confirmation and graduation. In your church display photos of them active in their natural settings—at home, school, activities, work, and community service.

6. Reflect with them on this message from St. Paul to Timothy:

   Let no one despise your youth, but set the believers an example in speech and conduct, in love, in faith, in purity....I am reminded of your sincere faith, a faith that lived first in your grandmother Lois and your mother Eunice and now, I am sure, lives in you. For this reason I remind you to rekindle the gift of God that is within you...for God did not give us a spirit of cowardice, but rather a spirit of power and of love and of self-discipline. Do not be ashamed, then, of...relying on the power of God (1 Tim 4:12; 2 Tim 1:5–8.

Chapter 10

HEALTH MINISTRIES

Real Snapshots, Real Times

Consider a farm couple who are caring people, working together with neighbors in haying and other shared chores in their farming community, and active in their Presbyterian church. On June 13, 1976, a typical summer day which threatens rain, they went into town for a church-mission planning meeting. During their absence, a powerful F5 tornado tore through the countryside, totally destroying a small village and then flattening the family's farmstead before moving on. They returned to find that everything they had worked for was gone. They thanked God for their safety, but their loss was devastating. Their small town church surrounded them with healing love, supplied them with needed clothing and provisions, and gave them use of a house in town. Through hands-on ministry they helped them slowly recover from their grief and stayed with them for the long run. The husband has passed away, but the wife has remained a pillar of strength in that church and community for many years.

Consider a farmer during the nineties, father of a large family, caring neighbor, and lay minister in his parish. The farm crisis of the eighties had stretched on, intensifying every farm family's worries about the future. One morning word came that his neighbor had been found hanging in the barn. He dropped his chores and ran over to help the shocked wife and children, staying with them as family and friends gathered to give support and to grieve. Over the next few months, he and his wife kept a supportive presence, but he noticed that the children were not coming over to their farm the way they used to to play with their children. The children were caught in shame and did not know what to do. He encouraged the mother to send them over. "You know," he said, "they have to have someone they can talk to—kids need to talk, and this is a safe place." *Barbara Pursey*[1]

Healing, Health, and Wholeness

Stories like this are multiplied all over rural America where caring people reach out to offer a healing hand and practical support for those whose lives have been shattered. Loving individuals, groups, and churches are the continuing presence of the healing of Christ as they work hand in hand with those who provide a needed range of public resources.

The qualities of healing, health, and wholeness are rich signs of spirituality. Jesus came "that we may have life and have it to the full." Wholeness is the dynamic well-being of body, mind, and spirit within a person, well-being with others and the natural world, and well-being with God. "Human beings are not just physical but also emotional and spiritual beings," said Charlotte Halverson, coordinator of Rural Outreach for Mercy Medical Center in Dubuque, Iowa. "When one is suffering, the other parts suffer too."[2] Wholeness/holiness is based on gratitude for life. It is compassion for what is injured, grieving, disconnected, downhearted, shamed. It is an active love for self and others. John the Baptist's question about whether Jesus was the Messiah yielded a surprising and quite concrete answer. "Go and tell John what you hear and see: the blind receive their sight, the lame walk, the lepers are cleansed, the deaf hear, the dead are raised, and the poor have good news brought to them" (Matt 11:4–5). Jesus' healing restored people's dignity and their place in society. His ministry, which he passed on to his disciples, was to restore people to full life physically, spiritually, and relationally. In the view of Scripture, the main goal of healing is not simply cure of disease but the presence of *shalom*, God's peace.

Rural communities have an experiential sense of that. Traditionally, people in trouble, if they ask for help at all, do not turn to professionals but to each other and their churches. They seem to know that body, spirit, and relationships are interrelated, and that the healing they need will not happen to them alone in a hospital or alone with a consultant. And those around them also know that healing will happen best when community care is apparent. One friend connects them with services, another spends time listening over coffee, kin take care of the children for a while, the pastor or parish nurse brings spiritual insight and solace, congregation members start a prayer chain, people help with needed work. All of this says, "We care, you are important to us, we want you to feel God's presence through us."

This Season of Rural Life

In December 1998, the National Association for Rural Mental Health, the State of Nebraska, and the Center for Mental Health Services convened a national summit on the "Farm Crisis and Mental Health: Then and Now." The presentations and summary report of that summit are valuable to our consideration of health ministries because they describe the season that rural life has been in through the 1980s and 1990s, continues to be in into the millennium, and is predicted to remain in for an unforeseeable length of time. In a background presentation, Roger Williams of the University of Wisconsin reviewed the last decade's distress factors related to weather and consistent low prices for milk, beef, hogs, corn, soybeans. He reviewed the changes affecting the rural community: business failures on Main Street, urban malls and national chains, shift in shopping allegiances, out-migration of local youth, rising age structure locally, school/hospital/factory closings, reduced volunteer involvement, and the health and human services squeeze.[3] Another presenter added: "I'm dealing as much with plant closings and layoffs.... The folks that are employed in those industries—many of them are from farm families. They took those jobs as a way of getting through the eighties."[4]

Williams observed that, in this extreme situation, the values and beliefs of this strong rural tradition can work against them. Rootedness may limit their vision for the future. The work ethic may make people work harder, but in exhaustion they may not work smarter. Their self-reliant spirit may limit people to their own resources alone. Their privacy in communication may keep them from sharing problems, and their attitude regarding help may keep them from reaching out to available resources. Traditionalism may keep them from considering change. Male and female roles are also disrupted as men feel less able to be provider and protectors, and the women's roles expand in the world leaving them less time to be nurturers and the "glue."[5]

It will not do to say to farm families, "Why not give this up and find something else?" Roger Hannan of the Farm Resource Center in Illinois ponders this dilemma with respect. "How do you explain the attachment to the land? How do you make sense out of refusing to give up a career racked with stress, debt, hard work, and uncertainty?"[6] That is how deep rural life and rural spirituality is.

This fierce passion blocked from success by factors beyond farmers' control can play into workaholism. Work, work, work is all the wives hear, plus don't spend any money! Is this a virtue or a vice? Is it devotion or addiction? asked South Dakota psychologist Val Farmer of the rural readers of his column. It turns bad, he answered, when it insists on perfectionism and suppresses feelings. "The difference between a workaholic and a hard worker lies in the amount of attention paid to other important things" (wife, family, friends, outside interests, community). This is a danger even in good times, he adds, because work is a rural value and farming is highly rewarding—one can see accomplishment and feel the interactive connection with living systems.[7] It stirs the spirit. But in getting out of balance, it feeds anger and exhausts resilience.

Spiritual Crisis

At the national mental health conference in Nebraska mentioned earlier, Judith Bortner Heffernan, Executive Director of the Heartland Network for Town and Rural Ministries, United Methodist Church, told a poignant story. She was interviewing farmers in relation to the crises of the eighties when the next-to-last farmer spoke up. "You have not yet asked me the right question." "What question should I have asked you?" she replied to the fifty-something farmer who had lost his farm. He did not form the question but he answered: "I feel God has abandoned me."[8]

The farm crisis, Judith observed, was originally called an "economic" crisis; later a "sociological, psychological, and emotional crisis" as well. But after she and her team presented their research, the conclusion was that the farm crisis was at its core also a deep "spiritual" crisis. Loss of the family farm for some also meant "losing the 'sacred' place where they encountered God and losing their major way of relating to God with whom they felt they worked in partnership to preserve the land and feed the hungry of the world."[9] It is important for pastoral ministers to understand that this spiritual crisis does not so much relate to formal religious "beliefs." For many, this kind of loss threatens their fundamental meaning, their understood sense of "covenant," and years of faithfulness. Return to wholeness will take time, care, and the healing grace of life itself.

Psychological and spiritual depression can be and often are more than individual. They can affect a whole family, congregation, or community. The spark is lost and the energy for doing things is missing. Pastors are vulnerable to taking that heaviness in. Reverend Judith Dye, a rural pastor in Nebraska, shared with the gathered professionals her experience as a clergy person in a rural community and as a hotline responder, and what it is to "be the container of collective community anxiety, coming home all jelly inside." "When the community is under anxiety," she said, "I feel myself pulling in. And you as caretakers, no doubt, have that same experience. That is to say, we as clergy and you as mental health folks need to be on the team together because we need each other bad. I need you folks out there, and I want you to know I'm out there to be there for you."[10]

Working and Caring Together

"Sustaining hearts" is about sustaining the hearts of the hurting, sustaining the hearts of the helpers, and sustaining/maintaining help over a long period of time. The chronic crisis and prospect of it continuing means that there must be great care in building networks and systems that can weather diminishment of funding, worker strain, and a milieu of discouragement. "Already," points out Joan Blundall, Associate Director of Seasons Center of Community Mental Health in Spencer, Iowa, "the financial margins have atrophied to the point that the mission of helping services has recognizably diminished probably thirty percent of what it was in the eighties."[11] She cited the research of Dr. Joanne Mermelstein, University of Missouri-Columbia, School of Social Work. Mermelstein indicates that ad hoc efforts for developing service systems never become integrated into routine operations and are lost when sponsorship ends. Many community projects of good will have experienced this. Local leadership and individual members cannot continue their efforts without what she calls "vertical leadership across all service systems" to develop services that could remain ready to respond to new waves of crisis without overstressing the local paraprofessionals.[12]

This is why the Heartland Conference in Nebraska was an inspiring and practical event. The sharing of professionals and church people modeled what is or needs to be going on statewide and regionally, building the necessary systems, sharing resources and teaching skills, sustaining the spirit for caring ministry. They are also trying to meet one of the biggest challenges—that of connecting those in need with the services that can help them. Since farm families are reluctant to seek services, especially regarding mental health and spiritual issues, outreach may need to be able to deliver the service on their own turf, their homes. Some programs locate staff in primary care clinics, extension offices, legal aid offices, community colleges, and social service agencies. Some provide "vouchers," so there is no cost. Some use "stress" titles rather than labeling it "mental health." Many give training workshops for clergy and lay leaders, as well as for "natural helpers" such as veterinarians, milk inspectors, livestock haulers, machinery dealers, creditors, cooperatives staff. In the eighties, church groups leading supportive and healing retreats moved around and held retreats over a wide area because people often were reluctant to participate where they were well known.[13]

Joan Blundall concluded her presentation with this reflection: "It is not the same as another job or another income. Remember, it's connective spirit, it's connective tissue that involves the head, the heart, the soul....We're not going to weep about the structures and the money not being there....So people, hopefully, if we're doing things right, we'll be in church basements. We'll be having trainings with hairdressers and bartenders....And kitchen tables will become more familiar than our desks. And when people ask us what we're doing and why, we won't be able to give them a quick answer, but we'll know."[14]

Churches: Signs of Life

"There is a feeling of terminal illness in our South Dakota town and in our small church," said Mary Hayenger, a farmer in Andover. "How do we help a community move through the stages of grief to acceptance and hope?" Her answer was powerful. "We begin by noting life signs. We have some people and each has special gifts. We have *some* money. We have *some* time. We have a building. There are people in the community—not as many as before but still some." She added this: "In Scripture and in modern times, God has done marvelous things with a few, with little, with the least. What is God longing for us to do with what we have?"[15]

Answers are happening, many in the form of health ministries. Congregations of faith offer almost unconsciously the ongoing positive community needed by all. They are the Body of Christ to each other, a supportive place in which to give and receive love. They are places of healing, places of familiarity and tradition, places of belonging, places of prayer. Reverend Karl Goodfellow, knowing the power of prayer, founded and directs the Safety Net Prayer Ministry. All over Iowa, and branching into other states, he matches people in congregations to particular farm families during the fatiguing and dangerous harvest season. He gives those who are praying, usually not farmers themselves, a prayer booklet to follow called *God's Harvest, God's People.* Each day of the six-week autumn period the devotions open with a Scripture, tell a rural story to help people visualize the life, and conclude with a short prayer. The farm people, knowing they are being prayed for and feeling the support, find their long hours under pressure less burdensome. They often report they are more careful not to push too hard. The safety record of families prayed for is very good.[16]

Alert congregations send their pastor and some of their members to the trainings offered by health and service professionals who are experienced in dealing with crisis and needs. Some congregations and church clusters look for root causes and work to support legislation that will benefit family farms rather than mega-farms and corporate interests. They support or nudge their judicatory and national church offices that teach and lobby for justice. They work out a way for follow-through with Action Alerts. And they fight for funding of social programs that are often the first to go in budget crunches, both in government and their own church bodies. A number of years ago a clergy advocate challenged our societal ethics when ten percent of the population was getting seventy percent of the health care; when 600,000 millionaires got social security benefits while 600,000 pregnant women got no prenatal care.[17]

In 1992, there were reports of three victims of sexual violence and the lack of services to confront the problem in a rural county in northwestern Illinois. But there were "life signs" in Vickie Gratton, a committed woman of faith. She got together "some people and some money and some time." A grassroots movement in JoDaviess County took hold. That brought together churches, community, and professional services to form Riverview Center in Galena. Today, they have offices also in Carroll County, Illinois and Dubuque County, Iowa. They are a spiritual life-sign to many.[18]

Parish Health Ministries

"Churches have a role to play in the physical well-being and welfare of their members," said Charlotte Halverson, who initiated the Parish Health Ministries program of the Mercy Health Center. "If you are physically ill or emotionally lonely, your spirit suffers."[19] The ministry is rooted in the churches' commitment to promoting wellness within the congregation and community. It is pastoral and also proactive in promoting physical fitness, mental health, social well-being, and spiritual strength—wholeness.

Parish Health Ministries' nurses are truly nurses. "If anyone had told me," one parish nurse said, "that I would renew my license at age sixty-six, I would have laughed. That is just what I did to become a parish nurse in our church and community."[20] In 1997 the American Nurses Association recognized parish nursing as a specialty with a standardized curriculum. Their parish function, however, is not nursing, but pastoral and educational. They serve as listener, educator, health consultant, volunteer coordinator, support group organizer, resource provider, and health screener. Some serve more than one church ecumenically.[21] They offer a competent and warm presence. They visit the ill to bring the prayers, well-wishes, and news of the congregation. They are good listeners. They help people understand their illness and treatment, translating in lay terms what a doctor may have told them quickly. Because many illnesses are related to stress and anxiety, they have a natural way of meeting and helping rural people in distress. This is an invaluable link.

A fitting tribute to the positive role that Parish Health Ministries plays in Iowa was a Proclamation for "Health Ministries Month" issued by the Governor Thomas J. Vilsack in 1999. In "whereas" form, it stated that:

- parish nurses and ministers of health serve the health and spiritual needs of thousands of Iowans throughout the state;
- parish nurses and ministers of health serve Iowans in their homes, in hospitals, and at care centers;
- the ministry is supported by Lutheran, Presbyterian, Disciples of Christ, Episcopalian, Friends, Methodist, Open Christ of Latter-Day Saints, and Roman Catholic denominations from congregations of all sizes.

The Governor therefore encouraged citizens "to support parish nurses and ministers of health in their congregations and in the important work they do serving the needs of Iowans."

Pastoral Response

1. Know the physical and mental health resources available in your area; some or many may be quite distant from your congregation or town. Place hotline numbers in

prominent places. Work with other churches or institutions in the area to create brochures listing resources and contact numbers and make them available for all at the entrance of the church or for ministry days. With a group of churches and some farm and town organizations, plan an area resource day; invite professionals to speak, bring exhibits, and be available for conversation.

2. Many service professionals are dedicated to their work because of their faith and Christian care. With other churches, plan a ritual or ceremony to show gratitude to them.

3. Consider having a parish nurse. This extension of personal contact with the ill and hurting is an outreach your congregation can offer. Seventy-two percent of Americans say they would welcome talking with their physician about faith, but most physicians feel uncomfortable with that. Parish nurses can fill that need.

4. Promote the biblical understanding of wholeness and holiness and God's call to the fullness of life. Reflect this in sermons and offer programs that promote health and wellness. Everyone in today's world will relate to programs on stress. If this is offered for all, you may make a safe place for those who most need to come.

5. Be an alive church. According to a *Newsweek* article, there is persuasive positive connection between faithful church service attendance and longer healthier lives, and good evidence for the protective effect of prayer.[22]

6. Consider connecting with the Safety Net Prayer Ministry, or setting up a similar way of praying for farmers in your own congregation (*snprayer@netins.net*).

7. Two videos may help: *The Connecting Link* and study guide have personal stories of how parish nurses carry out health ministries in their congregations. It is available

from the Center for Theology and Land (*www.ruralministry.com). Responding to Farm Stress* is coproduced by Mercy Medical Center–Dubuque/Dyersville and the Farm Bureau Federation. It is available from the Center *(halversc@mercyhealth.com).*

8. Read *Kitchen Table Wisdom* by physician and psychologist Rachel Naomi Remen, M.D. (Riverhead Books, 1996). In each anecdotal chapter she describes the challenges to and the power of the spiritual lives of terminal patients. Reading it may encourage helpers to empathize with people's struggles of suffering, faith, and meaning.

PART THREE

Dimensions of Church Life

This section of the book is a chance to look at church life more explicitly. We found once again that a quilt-like approach captures a number of dimensions of rural church: long-standing institution with members generous and resilient; a praying community of care; embodiment of the gospel, and voice spoken to the world.

We begin with writings from two contributors beyond our Rural Spirituality team: Donna Pinsoneault ("The Grace of It") and Reverend James Verkest ("Dying and Rising"). They capture the context of rural loss and yet the almost unexplainable spirit of abundance that keeps faith communities together and their spirits alive. We explore a variety of perceptions of "Who is Church," and the baptismal call of all Christians. With all of these understandings, and the sense of graced vitality yet struggle that was evidenced in Part Two, we provide a Pastoral Review for leaders.

The *Epilogue* following Part Three is both a calling and a sending. It is addressed as an "Open Letter" to all we have described in the rural quilt, the heartland's living community.

We are sent forth, in the spirit of Isaiah and the words of Jesus, "to bring good news to the poor...to proclaim release to the captives and recovery of sight to the blind, to let the oppressed go free..." (Luke 4:18). For we know that today, those words are indeed fulfilled in our presence, through the Spirit of God healing and enlivening all.

CHAPTER 1

THE GRACE OF IT

Type two key words into the computerized card catalogue at your local library: *rural life*. Within seconds the screen will flash titles for you, titles that can be roughly divided into two topics. The first set tells where to find books about quaint bed-and-breakfasts, quilt-making, vegetable canning, and front-porch pasture-gazing from whitewashed wicker rockers. The second directs you, without apology, to the section where the library has shelved its few volumes on poverty in America.

We are grossly under-prepared for the immediacy of the needs in rural areas!

As a human interest writer [Donna Pinsoneault, author of this chapter], I could simply pull together a story that asks, "Doesn't anyone see anything askew here—that people who live on fertile farmland go physically hungry? That people who live on land marked every few miles by century-old steeples may go spiritually hungry?"

And I am grossly under-prepared for the irony of hearing, nearly half a century later, words I heard over and over again from my grandmother, my parents, my uncles and aunts, during the few years of my childhood that we lived on the family farm. Times were hard then for the family, but that was not the story. The story was the seasons, the tilling, the planting, the harvesting; the saving of seed year after year, the incredible, unshakable, unquestionable faith in the will of God. And it occurred to me that the enormous challenges facing rural parishes today would not submit to being addressed solely through policy, sociology, strategic planning, or even theology.

There was a factor I could not name. So one Sunday morning I drove out to the parish I belonged to for a while as a child, to the church where I first heard about this Being called God.

The corn grows there right up to the edge of the parking lot, and I could almost smell the chicken frying as I stepped out of the car. My mother and aunt, along with other women of the parish, spent what seemed to me like days preparing for the summer parish picnics, dusting hundreds of plump pieces of milk-dipped chicken with flour, chopping dozens of cabbages into coleslaw while brown-sugared beans baked in black kettles in the ovens.

I wandered in the cemetery before Mass. Some of the stones were worn nearly smooth, the names indistinguishable. But others were clearly marked with the stout German family names I had heard so often, names of the women who had fried the chicken and the men who had tended the corn. Perhaps that's why the church itself seemed brighter to me on this visit. In fact, I sat bolt upright as the words of Isaiah rang out over the people and me:

> *On this mountain the* L*ORD* *of hosts will make for*
> *all peoples*
> *a feast of rich food, a feast of well-aged wines.*
> *(Isa 25:6)*

And the words of Paul followed:

> *I know what it is to have little, and I know what it is to have plenty. In any and all circumstances I have learned the secret of being well-fed and of going hungry, of having plenty and of being in need. I can do all things through him who strengthens me. (Phil 4:12–13)*

We are grossly under-prepared for the grace of it. For, while we struggle with questions of how to do this better; and

- while we rethink ministry;
- while we look to experts to find out what models are working;
- while suburban parishes begin to communicate with their rural neighbors about available family support groups and job search assistance;

- while we invite another parish council to share supper (or another parish to celebrate Eucharist) with us so we learn more about how to be church together;
- while we learn more about policy issues that will have an impact on the dinner table of every American;
- while we contribute toward scholarships for lay ministers who want to serve in rural parishes,

we cannot ignore the gospel, the gospel that speaks not of scarcity but of feast.

And as parish leaders walking with each other through this process of change, we can help each other focus on what we cannot yet see—new life surging through this branch. We can prepare with each other for the feast.

"The Grace of It," an article written by Donna Pinsoneault, Parish Leadership *newsletter, 1997, and shortened, with permission of the Archdiocese of Milwaukee.*

CHAPTER 2

DYING AND RISING

A Tale of Two Churches—Part One

For nearly 150 years this rural congregation has served the people of the area. It had sprung out of the frontier landscape in response to the planting of the seeds of the gospel by an itinerant pastor on horseback. Into the fertile hearts of sturdy farm folks and town residents the Word of God had found a home and the fruits of that planting took the form of a church, a faith community to worship God and reach out to God's people. The vitality once manifest in that faith community has by and large withered and become dormant in these later times. The once vital and vibrant congregation has become a church just seeking to survive in a culture that no longer nourishes it, but drains it of what little life it still possesses. Is there hope; is there opportunity? God has healed the lame and raised the dead. God can raise up the rural church as well. Its pastor prayed to Almighty God for a new vision, a new opportunity for life itself.

Vision and Revitalization

The context of rural ministry can often be summed up in the word *loss*. Yet in the midst of agricultural change, economic depression, aging population, and the fragmented culture of our times, there survives real hope and the assurance that God cares. Just as the seasons for planting and harvesting come and go, the church also goes through its seasons of vital life and dormancy. Just as the fields need to be revitalized to produce abundant fruits, so does the body of the church.

There are a number of ingredients necessary to transform a diminished or dormant church into a vital center of mission and ministry. Perhaps the most critical of these ingredients is a missional vision. Because the rural church context is often so consumed by loss and the fear of greater loss, the congregation turns inward. People in the church become concerned with "paying the bills" and lose their vision of being a God-inspired force for positive change. Budgets focus on "getting by" and supporting a limited program to meet the bare essentials of worship, Sunday school, and perhaps a women's group. The primary focus of ministry becomes member care and the trustees' budget. What is vision and how do you get it? That is probably the question that is on the lips of the faithful remnant that hangs on in discouraged rural churches today. They know that God is not interested in their just getting by, that God is not a God of the dead but of the living. God's vision is for inner spirit and fruits of ministry.

Power of Prayer and Community

When the disciples were not able to heal a person possessed, Jesus taught them the need of prayer. The congregation described above began with a small-group prayer ministry team of two or more people, people deeply committed to prayer and God's word. They prayed daily for their pastor, for their church, for their community. They prayed for renewal and new vision and then waited upon God's answer. They prayed for members with specific needs. They let everyone in the church know that there were people praying for them by name. They invited them to share their joys and concerns both corporately in worship and privately with the prayer team. And then they shared the miracles that inevitably come to the church committed to prayer.

Not only is prayer essential to renewal, so is community. One only needs to look at the life of the early apostolic church in Acts to see where life in the church comes from. The people of the apostolic church had so little and lived under such constant danger that they came to rely upon one another in their faith community for all their needs as well as their spiritual strength. They knew the power of sharing their faith as well as their very lives. Community was at the heart of the church in mission and ministry.

The rural church remembers community perhaps better than the urban/suburban church. This congregation found that despite change, community styles were deep in their memories and in their bones: sharing their stories, potlucks, and worship; knowing all their neighbors and tending to their needs; rejoicing in births and mourning the passing of community members. This was an antidote to the individualism of the times, a way of being church, not just going there on Sunday. They were more alive than they had thought.

A fresh vision for the church will almost always be centered in evangelism, extending to others the Good News. When the church saw itself as a vital link in meeting the felt needs of the community, it turned outward instead of inward. Community was more than just themselves. This broader outlook of faith provided resources for new and sustained vitality.

Rediscovering the Spirit in Worship

Jesus speaks of needing to be born again in the Spirit. He was answering a question about personal transformation, but it is just as true for the transformation of the church. God works through gifts of the Spirit. A vital congregation is one that seeks to identify not only God's unique vision for the faith community but also seeks to identify and empower those whose unique gifts of the Spirit will accomplish the mission.

In the story of this congregation, attention to worship and spiritual leadership helped revitalization and recapturing of the Spirit of God. It was not about contemporary versus traditional worship. It was about drawing out people so that they became more fully participatory. Inspiring prayer together filled the need to encounter God. The spiritual leadership of the pastor connected the congregation. Choice of inspiring worship music, well-prepared messages illuminating the biblical stories, and a church atmosphere inviting people to be part of the story in worship were necessary. A church with deep-spirited worship moves to respond to God's message through mission and witness.

Discipling and Spiritual Leadership

The rural church is a field ripe for harvest. For this revitalization to come to fruition, the people must be "discipled." Jesus set the pattern. As a congregation we gather the faithful, the seekers, and even the skeptics. In a prayerful small-group setting, people reflect and ask tough questions, learn to trust, are open to prayer, and finally, are mentored by others mature in their faith. The power of God's Spirit works through the study of Scripture and its application to life, strengthening faith communities that express themselves in servant ministry, building up churches that change communities and transform lives. There are churches that say, "If we only had a real leader for a pastor, things would be different for us." Leadership is a critical issue, but the pastor is not the only factor in church revitalization. Spiritual leadership comes from the combined gifts of the ordained leader together with people responding to their baptismal call. Both are known by the fruits of their faithful service. It is servant leadership, the kind of leadership demonstrated by Jesus himself, sharing vision that manifests itself in mission.

Paul knew that the primary role of the leader was to raise up more leaders if the mission was going to be accomplished. The congregation began to envision itself in Paul's image of the Body of Christ, recognizing the unique gifts each member of the congregation could offer to the work. Together they opened their hearts and minds through preaching of the gospel, the witness of their lives, practicing the spiritual disciplines, and most importantly, loving the faith community in the way that Jesus demonstrated his love.

A Tale of Two Churches—Part Two

That rural congregation, seemingly dormant, seeking only to survive, received a new vision. After that time of spiritual deepening and revival of outreach, a small group of faithful people voted to step out in faith and become a new church with a new vision. They did not reject their past, but learned from it. They bought a 10,000-square-foot building and totally renovated it into a home for the church and children's ministries. They committed to selling their old church, which had served their community on that site for over a hundred years, and to building a new worship sanctuary that would be accessible to all and inviting to the rising number of unchurched and under-churched of their community. They no longer believed that they were too small, or too poor, or too old, or all the other limiting words used to describe them and countless other small rural churches. Their vision of who they were was not limited because it was centered on God's power, God's abundance, and God's desire to do extraordinary things through very ordinary people. It was a church in transformation, not just change. It had become a church that looked forward to the future, not backward to what was once their church. There was anxiety, and not a few voices that said, "We can't do this." But with their eyes firmly focused on the vision that God had placed before them, they began to "cross the river" into the new land that had been promised to the faithful. There is a miracle in the making here, for this is a tale of two churches but of one faith community. They sought God's face and God healed their land (2 Chr 7:14–15).

Written for this book by the Reverend Jim Verkest, Pastor, United Methodist Church, Wisconsin Annual Conference (edited).

Chapter 3

CHURCHES INVOLVED

Story

Lois Swenson set up a booth at a county fair in southwestern Wisconsin. She hung a big banner that read "Food for Thought" and lured people closer by her friendly offer: "Would you like a taste of some organic cheese?" Lois is an activist, gardener, and Lutheran, a strong combination for engaging people in meaningful conversation. She showed the people an array of newsletters, flyers, and brochures about the plight of farms, increased concentration, the danger of factory farming, the importance of legislative efforts, plus movements in sustainable farming and direct marketing.

But it was the *church* flyers that consistently drew the most attention: "I didn't know churches were involved," many said, pleased but surprised. However, after talking with Lois, they left encouraged to talk to their pastors and congregation leaders to see if concern about food systems and rural issues could be made more visible in their home churches. Maybe they could host a table like this themselves, include quotes and notices in their bulletins, or perhaps start a church/community garden to provide fresh vegetables for their food pantries, or send some of their members to rural meetings and conferences to give witness to their concern, and create worship services that recognized both the harvest and pain of rural communities. There was energy in these conversations.

When We Say "Churches," Whom Do We Mean?

In situations similar to the one above, what do we mean when we say something like "I didn't know churches were involved"?

Perhaps sometimes we mean the official level, the Church Leaders in capital letters. But we should know that every mainline church body has studied rural and environmental questions from biblical, economic, pastoral, and ethical points of view and have promulgated statements, resolutions, or teachings on the side of dignity and justice for farmers, just-food systems that work for the common good, and proper earth stewardship that respects all of creation. Maybe we don't read, or maybe we want the leaders to engage the public and us in dialogue. Maybe we want them to be more vocal or to put the weight of their leadership behind the efforts of their own rural staff and task groups and encourage active participation in the issues.

Probably most people, when they use the word *churches,* are picturing their own congregation, pastor, leadership council, and general membership. Are they right in assessing that they are "not involved"? Do they hear sermons on Sundays about justice and earth stewardship? Is rural life—its seasons, hard times, and contributions—noted and prayed about in worship? Does the congregation council or social concerns group encourage a garden, study rural issues, send members to farm discussions or rural conferences sponsored by church-related organizations? Does the finance committee allocate a certain amount to support groups working on rural advocacy? There are many creative ways that local congregations and area ministerial associations are or can be actively and visibly "involved." Perhaps we underestimate the power of such witness to our own members and to the broader community.

Are We Forgetting WE Are Church?

Finally, when we say *churches,* how many think of *ourselves?* Somehow our sense of claiming this identity is weak if we instinctively think only of officials and our congregation's leadership. In fact, we are the church, the people of God. It is we, through our baptism, who carry the mission of justice and earth stewardship. As the prophet said, "There is no one to send but us." When we are involved, in whatever way, the church is involved. Our faith colors our decisions in work and the positions we take in public life. When we join others in movements for earth stewardship, call for fair prices, voice our objection to systems that threaten sustainability and the life of the community, we are doing so with the values our faith has taught us.

Involved—but Influential?

So, are churches involved? Yes, they are, at every level, but clearly they need to be more so if it is so hard to detect their presence and action. The harder question is: "Are churches an *influence?*" Important national and international "futurist" studies looking toward the new millennium said little about religion, and never took churches into account as a factor that could make a difference in their predictions about the direction the society would determine to take. That must give us pause. Are we a factor in shaping the direction of our communities, states, and nation? Are we, as churches, on every level truly taking on the rural/global issues of import today—sustainability, dignity, justice? Are we seen? Do we use our baptismal power? Are we an influence? That is the challenge of our call.

Chapter 4

PASTORAL REVIEW

Ministry is a shared vocation in the church, not simply something that pastors do. Pastoral leaders may help focus the ministry, but it is everyone's work. The gifts and graces of the Holy Spirit are generously shared with all. Part of the pastoral vocation is to identify and call forth the gifts of the people and equip them to be the light and love of Christ in all aspects of their life. The front line in ministry in the rural setting is not the church building, but the farm, the elevator, the town hall, the local store, the coffee shop, the home, the neighbor's barn. Gifted pastors and gifted people together will make a difference in rural life, even in crisis times.

1. As a rural church, work around rural life and rhythms in all aspects of its ministry. Timing is important for worship services, committee meetings, and farm visits. Settings are important for meeting people where they are, attending events that are important to the people. Being present communicates that the pastoral leader, and by extension the church, cares.

2. Realize that the "community of your call" is larger than your parish. It includes the whole web of the local and regional interrelationships of your people. That means your presence and support need to—in a planned way—extend to the larger community of organizations, churches, institutions, civic associations, services, and projects that are of service to all the people, and in which your parishioners are active. This is where the grace of God moves to form a people; this is where the vocations

of many contribute to the building up of the wider rural community of care, stewardship, and hope.

3. Study your "geography of faith." Pastors, who often come from outside the community, will need to become acquainted with the relevant issues in your area. Read rural journals, local papers, and organizational newsletters. This does not mean you have to become an expert in technicalities, but appreciative of rural hard work and sensitive to viewpoints and differences. Congregation staff and councils should also include in their meetings and ministry development shared study and discussion of the signs of the times in their area. Remember that the people are facing real cutting-edge questions of sustainability, dignity, and justice. Be there for support and guidance.

4. Listen and listen deeply to learn what is important to those you serve. Hear the sounds of the heart beneath the words they say. Listen to farmers, listen to their spouses and children. What is their dream; what is their pain? Listen to townspeople in agriculture-related occupations. Listen to service professionals and rural advocates. What are they dealing with? Listen for the cultural norms by which the people live. Listen for their operating theology that is likely to be expressed differently from formal theology. What is their understanding of who God is, and how God relates to the creation and to human beings? Listen to how they describe what is going on in rural life today. What are their hopes for the future? What does their farm mean to them? What has kept them on the land in spite of all adversity? How do they experience God in their lives?

5. Adapt your theological and spiritual approaches to rural/small-town life and the people's actual situations. This may mean modifying denominational resources that tend to have an urban flavor and may need rural nuancing. Build on the rural power of storytelling to communicate the truth of the gospel. Help in doing these things can be obtained from rural offices at the judicatory and

national levels, ecumenical rural-life organizations, and rural-oriented seminaries within the broader church.

6. Provide good theology and Scripture-based teaching and preaching. Keep your own learning fresh through reading, lectionary study days, and programs for pastors and other church leaders. Nourish in yourself compassionate ("God so loved the world...") and healing spiritual attitudes; strengthen your attunement to the gospel values of stewardship and justice. Ponder the meaning of Christian hope. Help your people avoid the punishment/reward approach to understanding their lives and relationship to God. Help them find solace against despair, strength from their deep faith, and alternatives to aggressive economic values. Emphasize gift, grace, mercy, newness.

7. Nourish a grace-filled and spiritually growing life yourself. This will sustain your heart in whatever is asked of you in your ministry. You are there to discover and nourish the spirit and spirituality of your members and the community you are serving. Be serious about ministry and concerned for others, but as one religion education teacher said to her colleagues, "Look saved!" Spiritual growth is fostered in others by helping them be more conscious of their own, and by modeling—truly believing in the presence of God and the workings of Grace among us. Deepen your own prayer life and pray with others. Weep with those who weep as well as rejoice with those who rejoice. Practice the rural disciplines of hard work, leisure, chats, and providential pauses demanded by weather. Seek opportunities for time with colleagues and retreat days. With the people, pray and make God a part of the life conversation.

8. Encourage the building of the faith community. Open and end all meetings of staff, congregation council, and committees with unhurried prayer that makes more than just business of their work together: "Where two or three are gathered, there I am in the midst of them." Worship that

grows out of the congregation's experiences of joy or sorrow affirms God's presence with them. The use of symbols out of everyday experience in worship can concretely connect people with their God. Formal Bible study and informal prayer/share groups are beneficial, especially if the idea originates in the congregation. Women tend to be more open to such semi-organized groups; the truck-stop coffee shop is a good place to converse with the men. Send some members to conferences or retreats that will broaden their experience of Scripture, theology, and spirituality. Creativity and genuine intent on the part of the whole congregation will be needed to draw in the youth, whose lives seem sometimes even busier than their parents' lives.

9. Much ministry is done in the daily rounds of rural life: conversations around a cup of coffee, across a farm fence, at the nursing home or the farmers market, responding to people in whatever is occurring in their lives, and reflecting with them about community news that affects them. It means getting to events and gatherings that are of significance to the people (celebrations, organizational meetings, field days, demonstrations, etc.). Spiritual ministry points people toward the spiritual significance of their relationships: with self, others, creation, and God. The pastoral leader helps people frame their situations in the light of God's Good News in Jesus Christ. A word of recognition and encouragement may be a lifeline. Be alert to what is going on, and help people deal with losses and griefs before they reach crisis point. Informal discussion and sharing times in people's homes may reveal a concern arising in the community. A prophetic voice for justice in a local issue may be required.

10. Finally, gift people with your love of rural life. You will find that God is very present. Nurture your own spirit with prayer and supportive companions in ministry. Sustain your heart and be sustained by the vibrant hearts of the people.

EPILOGUE

Call to the Table: Open Letter to the Rural Community

We have said that this book is a hymn of praise to the God who has so blessed the people of the heartland with grace and grit and a generous spirit.

Finally, this is also a call. We know what it is to be eucharistic people at the bountiful table of our God. We know the kitchen tables of our homes where we eat, plan, worry into the night, welcome kin and neighbors. We enjoy tables at the truck stop café, and set up tables for church and community commemorations and festivals. And today, when the stakes are so high, we know we must be at other tables too, tables of influence, tables where decisions are being made about "how things will be in this world." We need to be there to speak our truth from the spiritual place of our hearts.

We must be there. It is about our hearts and souls as people who care for the earth and each other. The questions of sustainability, dignity, and justice are urgent. Where we place our lives is of great importance. We must take back our right to describe "the real world" in the language of love, relationships, and spirit. It will make a difference.

We have a call to be cocreators, to work to keep alive the possibility of new vision in a society where it takes heart qualities of courage and commitment to think a new world into being. We have a call to do this in community. We are people whose traditions not only teach us about the common good but give us the interiority and practices of community to gather the people, as Jesus did, on the hillsides, in the meeting rooms, in front of the White House, and to know that we are not sheep without a shepherd but have the powers of leadership among us as we work together.

We are the people whose first holy words are "and God saw that it was good." That is the basis of our lives. The world is good and given to all. It is urgent that this vision of the world—as everyone's abundant gift—be the basis of our life choices and the ground from which we speak in our every sphere of influence.

We have a call because people are burdened and afraid—but resilient and creative beyond their imagining. Somehow in the midst of fragmentation, we have hope. You, our people of the heartland, are forces of hope because of the choices you make daily to keep land, people, spirit, and meaning uppermost in your living, nurturing, outreach and public involvement. You are the sustainers of heart.

Our hope is possible because we know that even though we feel we come to the table with only five loaves and two fishes, ours is a God of multiplication. Our hope is possible because God says over and over within us, "I am making all things new."

Miriam Brown, OP, editor

RESOURCES ONE: LECTIONARY OF THE SEASONS

I have discovered that there are seasons and rites for those who work the soil and work with the environmental creation. Some of these take on mystical qualities, while others seem more mundane in nature. With the evolution of time and technology, some of the traditions and activities are rapidly being lost with the stories of yesterday. I was not raised on a farm. When I received my first appointment in a rural church I took the time to listen and learn about the people that I had been called to serve. The following devotions are a reflection of simple truths and activities that have in some ways shaped my life.

The sequence of stories and devotionals seek to share some of the simpler activities that I have learned and observed through the years. By sharing them, my hope is that the reader may become a little more aware of the cycles of rural America. Reflection leads to understanding, and understanding leads to loving and appreciating the people and lifestyle in rural areas. If the readers' minds and hearts are open, then their journey in life and ministry in rural life will be a deeply rewarding and satisfying experience. *Reverend Karl Goodfellow*

Lectionary of the Seasons

Winter: Visit a Root Cellar

"Those who try to make their life secure will lose it, but those who lose their life will keep it." (Luke 17:33)

In our ultramodern age we take food preservation for granted. In our first parsonage, an old rambling house, there was a little room off to the side of the cellar. When I was being shown through the parsonage I was told that that was the root cellar. I didn't want to appear ignorant so I just nodded and we moved on by.

It was weeks later that I took the time to look closer at this room. It was walled off in a distant corner, away from the old furnace. Inside it was dark and foreboding. On its walls were neatly placed shelves, on the floor a number of bins that had a musty smell and dirt debris on the bottom. I was in the root cellar.

Through the coming years I learned that pastors, like everybody in the congregation, sought to be as independent as possible. That meant having a big garden, canning, and of course storing potatoes, squash, unripe tomatoes, fruits and vegetables. Stocking those bins and shelves became a labor of love. The girls helped carry in the squash and dig the potatoes, onions, and carrots. Then we would pick, wash, and wrap the last of the tomatoes.

I realize that there is considerable nostalgia that is associated with those early years of raising my family. Yet the smells and memories of the root cellar live on in my mind. The girls never complained about the vegetables we ate because they helped grow and harvest them. The potatoes were God's gift to us, because we found them in the garden—also a gift from God.

Prayer: God of our harvests, you have stored up for us a rich heritage, a feast. It has in some cases been placed there through the work of those who have come before us. It comes in our church, its traditions, the Scriptures, songs and liturgies. Give us wisdom in learning to feed upon this great store of eternal food. Amen.

Activity: Visit one of your older parishioners whose house still has a root cellar. Take the time to ask about what all was involved in putting up the supplies for the winter. Sit back and listen, enjoy, and fill your heart with the stories of yesterday. Then explore what is in the root cellar of your life that nourishes you through winter times of the soul.

Winter: See God's Blessing Poured Out; Winter's Snow and Rain Storms

> *Then afterward*
> *I will pour out my spirit on all flesh;*
> *your sons and your daughters shall prophesy,*
> *your old men shall dream dreams,*
> *and your young men shall see visions.*
> *Even on the male and female slaves,*
> *in those days, I will pour out my spirit.* (Joel 2:28–29)

When was the last time that your family spent the day together without a real agenda other than enjoying each other's company? You probably did a number of things, some together and some by yourself, such as reading, playing games, baking bread or cookies, or just relaxing. While pastoring in rural Wisconsin, when the storm warnings came out we ran to the store to stock up on milk and eggs, then put the car in the garage and settled in for a few days of being together. We all understood that once the storm hit we wouldn't be able to get out for a while so it was our time together as a family.

There are some blessings to be had in isolation. We have time to relax, play, and work on projects together. Having time together is good. Playing, working, and relaxing with family and friends bring healing to our souls and revitalization to our energy banks. Snowstorms are like unplanned holidays that are a gift from God and have sacred worth.

Being snowed in means that we are allowed to put all of our plans for the day on hold and we are given a blank sheet of paper to write anything on it we want. If you haven't had any homemade bread lately, or have a hankering for those cookies from a recipe that has been handed down to you, this is the day to make those things happen.

That game the kids just love to play and that you never seem to have the time to play with them, well, this is the time. Of course, there is an opportunity for an afternoon nap, or a short walk. (I love being out in the elements during a storm for just a little while.)

Prayer: God of wind and snow, you send us blessing in so many ways. At times you seem to interrupt our time schedules and give us some time out. Sometimes we become irritated by these interludes, when in fact you are pouring out special blessings for us. How stiff-necked we sometimes are. Make us sensitive to your Spirit today and make us flexible enough to understand your timetable is different from ours. Amen.

Activities: Start to gather the makings for your favorite recipes and have them on hand in preparation for that snow day. Help to build a sense of excitement into a walk during the height of the snowstorm. Maybe even build a snow hut by digging into a pile of snow. Remember, it is a day of adventure. And most important, make the time to take a few pictures of baking, game playing, and exploits into the snowy world. Someday you'll cherish those memories.

Spring: I Love Dandelions

> *God made the wild animals of the earth of every kind, and the cattle of every kind, and everything that creeps upon the ground of every kind. And God saw that it was good.* (Gen 1:25)

Have you ever wondered why God created dandelions? We spend millions of dollars every year attempting to eradicate them from our lawns. When it was time for the dandelions to sow their seeds I was delighted to find those little white balls of fluff that carried their winged seeds all over the yard when you blew on them.

I remember a sermon when the preacher brought in a shovel and trowel and he showed how he would dig dandelions out of his garden and yard. He talked about the depth to which dandelions sink their roots into the soil and that the only way of getting rid of them is to dig them out. Beekeepers have another view of dandelions. They are the first real bloom that feeds their bees in the spring. Bees embrace the dandelion bloom that produces a good supply of both nectar and pollen. This is a very important in helping to build the hive population in preparation for the work of pollination during the summer months.

Have you ever wondered what would happen if we could eradicate certain things from our environment that we don't personally like? The thicket in the woods with all the thorn bushes is the home of rabbits, songbirds, deer, chipmunks, and mice that find shelter and protection in its dense cover. Swamps, rather than being a nuisance, are a place where water is cleansed, and fish, waterfowl, and a host of insects breed and grow. Flooding, drought, snowstorms, forest and grass fires, along with disease are all a part of God's endless cycle.

This is true with the people in our communities, neighborhoods, and churches. Each of them is so different and yet very much alike. Learning to appreciate each of them, as the beekeepers love their dandelions, helps us to live and appreciate a fuller life.

Prayer: Each part of your creation, O God of rich diversity, has been placed there for a reason. The birds, bees, the worms, and snails all have a purpose. Even as you have created them for a purpose, make me sensitive today to the unique role you have created me to fulfill in the kingdom of God. Help me to grow, bloom, and sow your seeds in my season. Amen.

Activity: Take out a piece of paper and write the names of all the people that your life is dependent upon in your community. After each name write in what way you are dependent and what it would be like not to have a police force, dentist, teacher, snowplower, grocer, retired friend, waitress at the local restaurant, car salesman, or pastoral friend.

Spring: Life Is Like a Garden

> *And the Lord God planted a garden in Eden, in the east; and there he put the man [human being] whom he had formed.* (Gen 2:8)

In January many people will receive three things in the mail. The Publishers Clearing House sweepstakes packets, tax forms, and the newest editions of a variety of seed catalogs. The first two are usually set aside, while the seed catalog is taken to an easy chair for closer examination. The pictures and descriptions of beans, lettuce, cucumbers, tomatoes, potatoes, and beets are enough to make your mouth water. While Christmas may have its dreams of sugarplums, winter's dreams are of fresh fruits, vegetables, flowerbeds, and neatly manicured lawns. But spring is when the work begins.

It takes faith to make dreams become a reality. Learn about a person's dreams, their resolution to make dreams come true, and you will be able to predict their future. Some people will look at the catalog, even making the investment in seeds, and yet never get them planted. Others will order the seeds, get them planted, but will then let the garden go to weeds. Then there are those who will faithfully see the process through, allowing them to eat the fruits of their labors.

As many towns in rural settings are changing, it is our job to help people to dream, encouraging them to make the required investment that they need in order to make ends meet, while supporting them in striving toward making their dreams, personal and corporate, come true.

Prayer: Thank you, God, for the good earth, our brother sun and sister moon, the warm rain, and the seeds that you have given us to sow. Meet us in the midst our activities to allow us to dream well and to sow the good seeds of your kingdom. Amen.

Activity: Put on some work clothes and visit people working out in their yards. Assist them for shorts periods of time with any projects they may be in the middle of. While talking with them ask them to share the hopes and dreams related to the projects they are doing. Write these down on a piece of paper, and as you visit throughout the year, make sure to notice how their work is coming to fruition.

Summer: The First Tomato

> *Therefore the Lord himself will give you a sign. Look, the young woman is with child and shall bear a son, and shall name him Immanuel.* (Isa 7:14)

The Lord will give you a sign if you're a successful gardener, and it will be your first ripe tomato. It usually isn't the most perfect or succulent of the tomato crop. But it is the most talked about. People love to talk about signs. In each place that I've ever lived, there were people who lived, farmed, and gardened by the signs. Signs of the first or last frost; signs of a dry year or a hard winter; signs of an early spring or late fall.

These signs require observations of things, like where the black stripe is on the woolly caterpillar or how high up the stalk the ears of corn are situated, and then these observations can be related to future natural cycles. They are sometimes regulated by the moon or relate to Christian holy days. I know people who always plant crops that develop underground, like potatoes, on Good Friday. No matter if there is snow on the ground or not. They attempt to predict everything, from the weather patterns to who is going to be the next president. I'm not so sure how accurate these predictions are.

But finding people to share these bits of wisdom isn't hard. Simply ask some of your older people in the community and then listen. Learning to listen can be one of the richest sources of information about who people are and how they see themselves fitting into the bigger scheme of things. Signs help us to realize that in spite of our independence we are always involved with an interdependence on the times and seasons of life. It can be liberating to know that we are not an end in ourselves, and that there are forces we deal with that are beyond our control.

Prayer: O God, the fruits of our labors are sweet to us. Help us to realize that without your assistance we would be fruitless. You are the giver of the good seeds and earth. You send the rain and sunshine—and the earthworms that loosen the soil and help to feed the seeds we sow. We are lonely but connected, a small part of the vast creation that is involved in bringing that first tomato to fruition. Lord, thank you for the small part we play. Amen.

Activity: Do some asking around and see who is an authority on signs in your community. Most of the people will share some of the signs that they have observed. But usually there are a few that are keepers of the signs. Seek these people out and ask about the local lore of the land, weather, or river.

Summer: The Day They Dumped the Milk

> *The second angel poured out his bowl into the sea, and it became like the blood of a corpse, and every living thing in the sea died.* (Rev 16:3)

I believe in frugality. Work hard, save hard, and ultimately you will get ahead. This is the ideology on which rural life is founded. Our forefathers and mothers didn't come to this country looking for a free ride. They came looking for the opportunity to own a piece of land and build a life founded upon faith, strong family values, and hard work. What happens when these principles don't work?

Many times in the history of agriculture farmers have been asked, or rather told, that the commodities they worked so hard to produce were worth less than what they cost to produce. As an outsider it is hard for me to understand how farmers can spend two dollars to produce a bushel of corn, or X amount of dollars to produce a gallon of milk, and receive less than it cost to produce it. Any other type of industry could not last long by under-valuation of their products.

Today dairy farmers are dumping milk to protest milk prices that have again plummeted below their cost of production. Seeing dairy farmers pour out the fruits of their labor is like the bleak picture of death seen in Revelation. Creation is an expression of God's love and yet something just isn't right when things go amiss. Death, depression, and anger become an expression of meaningless servitude to economic and social systems that take advantage. This is not only true of farmers, but also of the marginalized caught in cycles of poverty.

It was a sad day when they poured out the milk. Their actions need to be understood as a statement about the unfairness of an economic system that keeps us caught in its clutches. Our prayers are with the disadvantaged and those who are caught in economic, social, and political structures of servitude.

Prayer: Just and compassionate God, you came into the world hearing the cry of the poor, destitute, sick, and socially disenfranchised. You have reached out, listened, and stood with them. Stand with us today as we your children reach out. Amen.

Activity: Take the time to visit a farm family and ask them to give you a crash course in farm economics. I believe that it will be an eye-opener and will help you to better understand life for those on the farm.

Autumn: Squash Hunt

> *"I am the vine, you are the branches. Those who abide in me and I in them bear much fruit, because apart from me you can do nothing."* (John 15:5)

There is nothing more delicious than farm-fresh produce. The yearly squash hunt can be a delightful and rewarding experience. During the growing year the squash plant sends it vines in all directions taking up as much of one's garden as it can reach out to. Shaded under the shelter of its leaves, developing squashes grow undetected to the casual observer. It isn't till the coming of the frost that the leaves die revealing the fruits of the plant's labor. This fall, see how many different kinds of squash you can find and eat.

It is a good time to make a special visit to an individual farmer's market or orchard to buy directly from the farmer—apples, squash, cranberries, grapes. Find some place with its own apple press and have some freshly squeezed cider. I can assure you that there is nothing like freshly squeezed cider. While visiting, you'll get a chance to meet the people who tend the soil and who find a sense of pride in the produce they grow.

Take the time to ask about the season, harvest, and their production. You might find that there are more varieties of squash, apples, and potatoes available than you realized. Taste some of the local honeys and find out what kind of flora was in bloom when this honey was produced. Gather some freshly harvested spices and use them in your fall cooking. Taking time and interest in your food and the people who produce it will enrich your appreciation of what you eat.

Prayer: God of abundance, the sweet taste of a squash is one small example of the love and blessing given to us freely. Even as we searched for the squash, allow us to search for the many blessings you desire to reveal to us today. Amen.

Activity: If you have gardeners/orchard keepers in church, ask them to bring in the fruits to church to place in the altar area. This helps us to see the connection between the work of our hands, as gardeners/farmers, and God's role in helping to produce a harvest.

Autumn: It's Just a Little Snow

> *"As long as the earth endures,*
> *seedtime and harvest, cold and heat,*
> *summer and winter, day and night,*
> *shall not cease."* (Gen 8:22)

It was the first real cold snap and snow of the season. There will be snow on the ground for deer season, and sledding, and if it continues to snow there is a chance that they will cancel school. For those all nestled snug in their homes it is a warm and close feeling. But for farm families who are still attempting to get crops in, stored, or hauled to co-ops or to the river, it can be an extremely dangerous time.

A few years ago I met a young man named Richard who deer-hunted with us. He was filled with smiles as we joked, ate, and tramped the woods together. As Sunday afternoon drew to closure a light snow mixed with rain started to fall. We rushed through the last drive and Richard told us that he needed to go to work the next day and help his dad get the rest of the corn moved during the week, so he wouldn't be able to hunt with us that week. That was too bad, I thought, because he was a nice addition to our hunting party.

The next day we canceled our hunting because the rain and snow had turned into a full-fledged storm. But Richard's father hadn't wanted to wait the storm out and had decided to move corn. According to Dan, my brother-in-law, the tractor Richard's dad was driving seemed to have hit a patch of ice and then went into a ditch and rolled over. It killed him.

I've learned that fall and the harvest season is a lot more than just getting the crops in and out of the fields. It's moving millions of tons of corn, beans, and other grains in weather that can be inclement and dangerous. Moving these crops before full winter can be one of the most dangerous seasons of the year. While Thanksgiving can be a day of joy, it can also be a day of sorrow as we reflect upon all those who have given their lives in order to get the harvest to our dining room table.

Prayer: God, weather changes and especially snow can bring many unseen dangers. Protect us when we are in a hurry, drive too fast, or misjudge how slippery it is. Send your angels to look over us as we attempt to work in the rain, ice, and snow. Amen.

Activity: Take time while saying grace to pray for all those who made it possible for you to eat the food on the table. From the cranberries to the whipped cream on the pumpkin pie, there were hands that tended, assisted in the growth process, harvested, and transported it to your table. Thank God for all these people.

RESOURCES TWO: PRAYERS AND RITUALS FOR SUSTAINING HEART

Over the years, the Churches' Center for Land and People has created prayers and rituals for many occasions. The following are a few samples easily adaptable for a variety of settings and occasions.

For Gatherings That Celebrate the Quilt of Rural Life

The following prayers can be used at the opening and closing of meetings, gatherings, or retreats that honor the rural-community quilt described in Part Two of this book.

Opening Prayer:

> *Convener:* We come together as quilters of our rural community.
> O God of community, who makes all things new,
> We thank you for your call to create new life together.
> May we bring listening hearts to our gathering and open minds that allow us to explore, question, and risk fresh ideas and dreams.
> We quilt with the pieces you have given us.
> We trust in the words you will speak to us this day through each other. Amen.

Closing Prayer:

> Dear God, quilt-maker of community, we give you thanks for gathering us, pieces of the rural fabric, together today. We give you thanks for being the

patternmaker of our quilt, the heartland. We give you thanks for being the thread that has united us in our decision-making. We give you thanks for being the single-piece backing that has held our communities together during times of crisis. We give you thanks for binding us together in a common place with common goals to serve the common good. We go forth from this place with renewed energy. May our fire be shared by all in our rural communities. May your work through us be displayed in vibrant colors everywhere we go. Amen.

For Farm Meetings

These opening and closing prayers may be preceded by and end with a hymn of choice. The right and left sides of the gathering could alternate lines.

Opening Prayer:

We stand before you, Holy Spirit, aware that we gather in God's name.
Come to us, remain with us, and enlighten our hearts.
Give us light and strength to know your will, and to live it in our lives.
Guide us by your wisdom, support us by your power, for you are God.
You desire justice for all: enable us to uphold the rights of others.
Unite us to yourself in the bond of love and keep us faithful to all that is true.

As we gather in your name, may we temper justice with love so that all our decisions may be pleasing to you, and earn the reward promised to good and faithful servants. You live and reign one God, forever and ever. Amen.

Closing Prayer:

Loving God, on this holy day we have laid before you our concerns for farm communities. We know the land is holy to you. We know the lives of your rural children are precious. We pray that your healing renewing Holy Spirit will move over the land and its people like a refreshing breeze. Cleanse your land and strengthen its farm people. Heal their hurts and give them new dreams. Give us the will to answer your call to community. Strengthen in us the sense of justice and mutual support. Give us the determination to work together in your name. Amen.

Blessing of Farmers and Gardeners

It is good for a congregation to bless its farmers and gardeners at the beginning of the planting season. Just before the close of a Sunday service, invite farm families to come up to stand in front facing the congregation. Ask the people to raise their hands in blessing.

Presider: God, you have created us in your image and further dignify us by making us coworkers with you in caring for your creation. We bring to you in prayer this day the farmers and gardeners you have entrusted to our community. We ask that you watch over them. Grant that their work may serve them today, and their children tomorrow. Give them a just return for their labor, and help them to be fair and compassionate to all. Let the rhythm of your creation teach them your divine wisdom. May your love make sacred their lives and their work. O God, we ask you to send your Spirit. Guide and direct them in the ways of your holy creation. Amen.

Presider: Go in peace to extend God's love into your living and working together.
All: Thanks be to God.

Congregational Ceremony for Rural Concerns

This ceremony can be adapted for occasions of special need or concern, such as seasons of planting or harvesting, or in times of weather-related disasters—floods, droughts, destructive storms.

(People enter a softly lighted worship space with a centrally placed lighted candle as a focal point. Nearby is a "tree" with branches from which people can hang names or petitions. Have ready some paper tags and pens, and ties or hooks. This tree can stand in the church for several weeks to be added to and visited prayerfully.)

Call to Worship:

Leader: The Lord is my light and my salvation; whom (or what) shall I fear?

All: The Lord is the stronghold of my life; of whom (or what) shall I be afraid?

Song/Hymn/Spiritual Song. Examples: Taizé song "The Lord Is My Light," or "O Lord Hear My Prayer."

Reading: Psalm 27

Listen for the word or phrase that speaks to you.

Silence for personal reflection.

Reflection by the leader (optional).

Petitions of the community (people speak their concerns, needs).

Group response: The Lord is my light and my salvation.

Ceremony of the Tree:

Invite people to write petitions on the tags provided. After time for writing, invite people to gather around the tree and to place their petitions prayerfully on the branches. Remain near the tree and sing together a well-known, meaningful hymn. If appropriate, invite people to share some of their prayers aloud.

Group Benediction:

Join hands in a circle. (Optional: One by one, say the person's name on your right and the blessing prayer: N____, the Lord is the stronghold of your life.)

All raise their hands toward the tree as the leader asks God's care and compassion in this special time of need.

For Sending of Rural Ministers

This is a reflective Prayer of Sending for both clergy and lay people who will be going forth in rural ministry. (The task can feel very big to those sent in the face of rural complexities today.)

Reading: Matt 13:31–32

"The kingdom of heaven is like a mustard seed that someone took and sowed in his field; it is the smallest of all the seeds, but when it has grown it is the greatest of shrubs and becomes a tree, so that the birds of the air come and make nests in its branches."

Reflection together:

Leader: The seeds we offer may seem small. With God's grace our seeds will grow to give shelter for many. Let us share our concerns and pray for the needs of rural ministry. *(Allow time for prayerful sharing.)*

Reading: (Luke 24:13–17)

On that same day two [of the disciples of Jesus] were going to a village called Emmaus, about seven miles from Jerusalem, and talking with each other about all these things that had happened. [Pause] While they were talking and discussing, Jesus himself came near and went with them....

(Invite prayers for those being blessed and sent.)

Closing Prayer:

Loving God, in the creative tension of ministry, gift us with: a sense of direction and commitment, respect for all with whom we will live and work, belief that our small seeds will grow, and we will be able to give shelter to those in need. May we trust in you who calls us and walks with us. We build on what has brought us to this time and place, and we trust in your saving presence as we ponder the gift of our ministry. Amen.

Opening Ritual for a Rural Conference or Day of Prayer

In an opening ceremony, have seven people bring forward, one by one, the chosen symbols of farm, family, churches, towns, cities, government, and the planet. With the symbols held high, they are brought in and placed on a special table near the altar or conference podium. (Young people, multi-generations, or other designated representatives can be chosen for this).

Presider: In this community of faith, we gather to face complex questions, to share hope and insights, to commit ourselves to the fullness of life for all. We bring (before the altar of God/to this place of honor) symbols of our lives. *(Bearers of symbols, pacing themselves, begin to move forward as their part is read).*

Let us ask God's blessing on our *farms,* praying that we may respect all life and be caregivers of the earth as we work with the land to bring forth nourishment for the heart; on our *homes,* where we first learned the vocation of stewardship, where we plan and worry and make decisions day by day, where we take strength in each other and the trust God has given us; on our *churches,* where in faith-filled community we are strengthened by God's Word and sacrament, where our gifts are offered, blessed, and broken, given in love for others; on our *towns* and *cities* where we create vital communities of relationships, and connections of town and country in our food systems; on our *government* and our public life as citizens where we put forward our values to choose good leaders and influence legislation that will promote the common good; and on our *globe,* blue-jeweled planet, home of the intricate biocommunity of life, amalgam of nations not yet wise about living together; sacred trust, holy ground.

(Close the ceremony with a hymn of choice.)

Ceremony to Honor Rural Mission

Churches, organizations, institutions, farms, co-ops, service agencies, all have Statements declaring their Mission. Hearing these read aloud within a reflective setting is powerful. Invite these groups to bring their statements to proclaim in a ceremony as part of a retreat or conference.

Reading: (Luke 4:16–21) (It would be good to have a young man around Jesus' age read this.)

> When he came to Nazareth, where he had been brought up, he went to the synagogue on the sabbath day, as was his custom. He stood up to read, and the scroll of the prophet Isaiah was given to him. He unrolled the scroll and found the place where it was written: "The Spirit of the Lord is upon me, because he has anointed me to bring good news to the poor. He has sent me to proclaim release to the captives and recovery of sight to the blind, to let the oppressed go free, to proclaim the year of the Lord's favor." And he rolled up the scroll, gave it back to the attendant, and sat down. The eyes of all in the synagogue were fixed on him. [Pause] Then he began to say to them, "Today this scripture has been fulfilled in your hearing."

Hymn: "We Are Called to Act for Justice" (or another hymn about mission)

Mission Statements:

Representatives form lines at two microphones at the front. One by one and alternating, they proclaim their groups' Mission Statements.

Refrain at the end of the Mission Statements: We are called to act for justice.

Closing:

All participants form a circle. Personal statements or prayers are invited (e.g., "I am called to...," "My mission is to...").

(Choose a closing hymn of Thanksgiving.)

Renewal of Commitment to Rural Community

Although this prayer uses the Call Statement of the Churches' Center for Land and People (beginning at "This we share"), the words are appropriate for any quilt-like gathering for remembering our bonds and renewing our commitment to one another.

Presider: God of land and people, on this holy day we have laid before you our concerns for our rural people, and our gratitude for your ever-enlivening presence. Give us the will to answer your call to be church and community in your holy land. Renew in us a sense of justice and hope, as we work with others for the well-being of the rural community in this, our geography of faith.
All: Amen.

Together:

This we share:
towns + land + schools + history
problems + hopes + faith + future
and the presence of God among us.

We see the need
to pray
to think + to support + to respond
to encourage + to embolden + to empower
to stimulate + to study
to rejoice + to celebrate
to be together.

We covenant
to strengthen and build upon
our common bonds.

THE RURAL SPIRITUALITY TEAM

The Preface and Introduction describe the breadth of inquiry and interaction that makes this book authentic and alive. Each of the six members of the Rural Spirituality Writing Team did truly author this book through our seeking, contemplating, and bringing to word the life of the Spirit in the people of the heartland. If people are going to "write by committee," a better group could not have been found—mixed in background, experience, and points of view; ecumenically rich and open; all engaged in listening, coming to the table with insight, committed to the task, and best of all, wonderful to work with.

Miriam Brown, OP, came from a "back to the land" family of the fifties. As a Sinsinawa Dominican sister, she has taught many years, directed college human issues education, developed programs and networked in a diocesan pastoral center, given retreats and demonstrated for social justice. From 1989 to 2003 she was the executive director of the Churches' Center for Land and People (CCLP), linking churches and organizations, gathering people annually to share their spirit and strengthen bonds, coordinating working committees on earth stewardship, ethics, renewal—and co-coordinating the rural spirituality group which has produced this book. Miriam contributed her knowledge and appreciation of the heartland's network of spirited and spiritual people as especially reflected in Parts Two and Three. She brought the language of the six writers into one voice and prepared the manuscript for publication. She continues ministry in adult spirituality.

Rev. Dr. Barbara Pursey is an ordained Presbyterian minister and retired associate professor of spiritual formation and faith education from the University of Dubuque Theological Seminary. Her interest in rural issues and spirituality began when she and her husband moved to Iowa in 1964 and her commitment deepened while on the faculty of UDTS. She served on the advisory board for the seminary's Center for Theology and Land (a shared ministry with Wartburg Seminary) where she led workshops on rural spirituality at several annual conferences, as well as at CCLP's rural life gatherings. On retiring she took up the challenge to explore rural spirituality and Miriam Brown joined her as cochair. Barbara helped move the group along with an undaunted spirit, contributing her theological mind and love of Scripture. She studied what we were bringing to the table and contributed much to Part One's distillation of themes and characteristics.

Rev. Karl Goodfellow, an ordained United Methodist minister, has been a rural-church pastor for many years. He is presently pastor of the Preston/Sabula UMC churches in Iowa. He serves his area in ambulance service, is a speaker for rural life and prayer ministry, and has served on the UMC Iowa Conference Boards of Evangelism and Discipleship. After completing his doctorate in ministry, he founded and is director of Safety Net Prayer Ministry that involves church members in praying for farmers during the hazardous harvest season. He produces a new *God's Harvest and Ministry* booklet each year (nine so far) with daily devotions for the six weeks. Karl always came to our process meetings with zest and insight for the task. With his ear for rural stories and a heart for their inner meaning, he created the "Lectionary for the Seasons" for the first resource section of the book.

Rev. Diane Jochum is an ordained minister in the Presbyterian Church USA, residing in Freeport, Illinois. While pastoring a small rural congregation for eight years, she helped form the Family Farm Task Force of Blackhawk Presbytery in Illinois in support of small rural congregations, and moderated until 2004. Through the task force she initiated collaborative forums for presentations and sharing of resources in relation to the farm crisis, and created a base of relationships for the area to build on. She facilitated workshops in spirituality at church-related conferences to invite people to reflect on the rural-spirit connection. Her present ministry is spiritual guidance, retreats, and hospice chaplaincy. Diane was a reflective presence on the writing committee. She contributed her insight into the spirit of congregational life and her sensitive creativity in prayer and ritual.

She helped us with her calm skills of facilitating when our work got complicated or discouraging.

Ambrose Koopmann has farmed all his life in eastern Iowa, raising a large family and now, working with two grown sons, continuing with a small dairy herd and their new enterprise, goats. Interested in rural life and ministry, he came to one of CCLP's three-day "Orienting to Rural Ministry" programs in the early nineties; because of his experience and sensitivity he became a member of the presenting team for several years. He studied with the Archdiocese of Dubuque to become an official Lay Minister and has organized a number of evenings for rural churches, himself speaking of rural spirituality. Ambrose brought to the writing team the humility and authority of one who has lived it all—farming, losing, regaining, and working with his sons. His stories are real and caring, his faith deep. It is clear why his teenage daughter chose to write about him as the one who "left footprints on her heart."

Larry Tranel grew up on a farm and lives with his wife and their six children on a small dairy farm in southwestern Wisconsin. He earned BS and MS degrees in agricultural economics and international studies at the University of Wisconsin-Platteville. For ten years he worked with the University of Wisconsin Extension and has now been six years with Iowa State University Extension as Dairy/Beef and Forages Field Specialist. He ministers in his rural church with music, youth, and the marriage preparation program, and is an ordained deacon in the Madison Diocese. He has collaborated with others on farm family relationships and profitability; his work with CCLP is recognized by Extension as part of his outreach work. He carries in himself a strong sense of vocation—in family, farm, community, work, and church. He brought to the group his experience of belonging to a faith-filled farm family, as well as the possibilities of working within an institution.

NOTES

We would like to have written more about each of the good people whose names are listed in these endnotes, but that would be another book, so we worked some of the information into the text itself. *CCLP* refers to the Churches' Center for Land and People.

Part One: Rural Spirituality

Chapter 2: Rural Spirituality

1. Anonymous, by choice.

2. JoAnn Pipkorn, "Sixty Acres," delivered at Churches' Center for Land and People (CCLP) Rural Life Gathering, October 2000. (See story opening Chapter 2 of Part Two.)

3. John Kinsman, "Global Corporations Squeezing Family Farmers Worldwide," *The Capital Times (*Madison, WI), September 6, 2000. Family Farm Defenders: *www.familyfar-mdefenders.org.*

Chapter 3: Themes in Rural Spirituality

1. Janet Kassel, quoted by Brian Lavendel, "Faith-Based Conservation," *Conservation Voices,* October/November 2001, p. 9.

2. The following seem to be general understandings of the terms about farms in the heartland. *Traditional/conventional*—independent, medium-sized family farms including combining/incorporating farms within a family for extended acreage needed today; diminishing diversity and rising costs for probable use of chemicals and bioengineered seeds for row-crops and antibiotics for animals; family committed to the land for generations. *Industrial*—mega-farms, often with factory-farm style, buying supplies from beyond the local area, prescribed use of chemicals and antibiotics, and contracting to work for a major corporation with the advantage of being connected to processing and marketing. Integrated into the agribusiness system. *Alternative*—usually

smaller farms or gardens. Most are organic, or close to it, even if not licensed; direct marketing to avoid the larger systems; emphasis on soil health, simple lifestyle, and people networks.

3. Michael Reicherts, quoted by Jane Logan-Kuebler, "Switch to Ridge Till Required 'Attitude Adjustment,'" *Iowa Farmer Today,* February 23, 1991.

4. Roberta Hinman, in *God's Harvest, God's People,* 1995, Rev. Karl Goodfellow, editor.

5. Gary A. T. Guthrie, "The Spirituality of a Farmer—Working Eucharist Holy Ground," *The Ecumenical Ship,* newsletter of the Ecumenical Ministries of Iowa, August 2002, p. 4.

6. Kassel, p. 4.

7. Greg David speaking at a CCLP Rural Life Gathering, October 2002.

Part Two: The Heartland

Chapter 1: The Land

1. Jan Libbey, "I Am of Here," *Women, Food and Agriculture Network Newsletter,* February 1998, reprinted with permission. Jan listened to an older woman who was being urged to move from the farm to town. She captured the spirit of the woman's response in this poem.

2. Ambrose Koopmann, see "Rural Spirituality Team," p. 172.

3. Bob Kliebenstein, "The 'Other' Family Member," *Tomah Journal,* August 12, 2002.

4. Walter Brueggemann, Chapter 4, "Reflections at the Boundary," *The Land,* Philadelphia: Fortress Press, 1977, p. 45ff.

Chapter 2: Families

1. Pipkorn (the story opening Chapter 2 of Part Two).

2. Larry Tranel, see "Rural Spirituality Team," p. 172.

3. Beth Waterhouse, speaking to college students of the Higher Education Consortium for Urban Affairs (HECUA), December 11, 2003.

4. *The Farmer's Wife,* a David Sutherland film, *PBS Frontline,* September, 1998.

5. Sue and Ron Visker, described and quoted by David Hanners, in "Rural Life at Risk," Part Two of a series titled "Harvest of Risk," *Saint Paul Pioneer Press,* July, 1999.

6. Rev. Karl Goodfellow, "Social Implications of Creating a Prayer Support System for Farm Families," delivered at a Behavioral Health and Safety Conference, May 29–30, 2003, Kansas City, Missouri. See "Rural Spirituality Team," p. 171 *(snprayer@netins.net).*

7. Neil Hamilton, "Bigger Isn't Everything," *Des Moines Register,* October 25, 1999.

8. Mark and Rita Mays, farm family in Iowa, speaking at a CCLP Rural Life Gathering, 1990.

9. Sandra Simonson-Thums, lay Rural Outreach specialist (715-427-3779).

10. Ron Hanson, University of Nebraska-Lincoln agribusiness professor.

11. Roger T. Williams *(rwilliams@dcs.wisc.edu).*

12. "The Unseen Landscape: A Necessary Discussion," study sheet, CCLP Ethics Committee.

Chapter 3: Rural Congregations

1. Rev. Diane Jochum, see "Rural Spirituality Team," p. 171.

2. Rev. Leo Maxwell Brown, as described for this book.

3. Story retold in *Clippings,* newsletter of CCLP, Volume 11, Number 4, September-October 2000, p. 3.

4. Quoted by Rev. Bill Cotton, "Laity Seeking Seminaries," *United Methodist Rural Fellowship Bulletin,* Summer, 2001, p. 6.

5. Janet Kassel, speaking during CCLP Earth Stewardship Committee meeting.

6. Rev. Dan Dibbert, presently pastor at Bethany Lutheran Church, Mauston, Wisconsin.

7. Christine Feagan, OP, Hispanic Ministry, St. Mary's Catholic Church, Marshalltown, Iowa.

8. Tom Harkin, Senator of Iowa, quoted by Lyn Jerde, "Father White, Farmers' Friend Dies," *Telegraph Herald* (Dubuque, IA), August 29, 1996.

9. Rev. Richard Whiteing, "'Big Pork' Comes to Town," *Catholic Rural Life Journal,* Spring, 1999.

10. Judith Heffernan, quoted in *Rural Ministry*, Nashville, TN, Abingdon Press, 1998, p. 21. Phone: 573-882-7232.

11. Rev. Kathy Gerking, *"Greatest Power Is in the Touch of Jesus,"* Southeastern Iowa Synod, Evangelical Lutheran Church of America (ELCA), February 1999, p. 3.

12. "To Get the Discussion Started," study sheet, CCLP Ethics Committee.

Chapter 4: Family Farming

1. Rev. Tom Biatek, United Methodist Church, Iowa Conference, contributed the story for this book.

2. Leigh Ann Koopmann, "Foundations," September 20, 2000, at age 16, about her father Ambrose Koopmann.

3. Phil Hueneke, as told in CCLP Earth Stewardship Committee meeting.

4. Sandra Menefee Taylor, *Minnesota Food Association Digest,* April 1997, p. 2.

5. Tranel, "Farming in the Heartland" (title missing), November 2000, p. 2.

6. Tim Kapucian, quoted by Jerry Perkins, "Farmer Takes Leave of Land for Hope of Work in Town," *Des Moines Register,* November 25, 2001.

7. Joel Greeno, quoted by Tony Ends, "Four Men Answer the Same Call," *The Janesville [Wisconsin] Gazette,* July 31, 1998.

8. Keith Wold, "I Remember," written for this book, 1998.

9. Dick Poppen, tentmaking pastor in South Dakota, quoted by Evan Silverstein, "Farmers Struggle to Keep the Faith," *Presbyterians Today,* November 1999, p. 13.

10. Doug and Trish Scheider, "Mission Statement," Scheidairy Farms Inc., northern Illinois. Read in panel at a tri-state church conference, "In a Global Economy, Who Profits?" Dubuque, Iowa, June 17, 2002.

11. John Ikerd "Hallmark of the New American Farm," delivered in Ames, Iowa, January 5, 2000. *(www.ssu.missouri.edu/faculty/jikerd)*

12. James Goodman, "World's Farmers Stand in Solidarity against WTO," *The Capital Times* (Madison, WI), October 29, 2003.

13. Williams, "The Farm Crisis Continues: Pastoral Leadership in the Church," presented for CCLP "Bishops' Day," October 14, 1994.

14. Richard Cartwright Austin, "Moral Creativity: God's Challenge for America," *Earth Matters,* Summer, 1989, pp. 9–12.

15. Website: *www.elca.org/dcs/economiclife*

Chapter 5: Alternative Movements

1. Rev. Sherrie Lowly, Sunday Bulletin, Galena First United Methodist Church, July 2000.

2. Richard Pirog, *Food, Fuel, and Freeways,* Leopold Center for Sustainable Agriculture, University of Iowa, Ames, June 2001.

3. "Finding Food in Farm Country," Community Design Center, 2001; cited by Dana Jackson in "Food Network Finds Food in Farm Country," *The Land Stewardship Letter,* April/May/June 2003, p. 16.

4. Kassel, in CCLP "Soil and Spirit" conversations.

5. *Against an Infinite Horizon: The Finger of God in Our Everyday Lives* by Ronald Rolheiser, OMI.

6. Earnie Bohner, Missouri farmer, quoted in sidebar, *Sustainable Agriculture Network,* November 1999, p. 5.

7. Joe Paddock, Nancy Paddock, Carol Bly, *Soil and Survival,* San Francisco: Sierra Club Books, 1986, p. 52.

8. Fay and Skip Stone shared this with us for this book.

9. Bill Welsh, "The Day the Welsh Family Farm Turned Around," *Heartland Portrait,* Robert Wolf, editor, Free River Press, 1995, pp. 85–88.

10. Rita and Ralph Engelken, *The Art of Natural Farming and Gardening,* Greeley, Iowa, Barrington Hall Press, 1981.

11. Kinsman, *www.familyfarmdefenders.org.*

12. Greg Welsh, "The Way Back," *Heartland Portrait,* pp. 88–91.

13. "Cleveland Symposium Report" summarized by Paula Vargas, in *Politics of Food,* September-October 2002, p. 8.

14. Upper Midwest Organic Farming Conference, sponsored by the Midwest Organic and Sustainable Education Service, Inc. (MOSES). *(www.mosesorganic.org)*

15. Tony Ends, "New Resolve, New Leadership, New Project," *Voices,* newsletter of CCLP, Vol. 1, No. 1, December 2003, pp. 1–2. Partners in Stewardship is a project of CCLP, Illinois and Wisconsin Collaborative Regional Alliance for Farmer Training (CRAFT), the CSA Learning Center in Caledonia, Illinois, and Michael Fields Agricultural Institute in East Troy, Wisconsin.

16. Walter Brueggemann, *Prophetic Imagination,* Philadelphia, Fortress Press, 1978, p. 44.

17. Rita Placke, quoted in "Organic Farming: The Correct Choice for the Plackes," by Charley Preusser, *The Platteville [Wisconsin] Journal,* December 13, 2003.

Chapter 6: Grassroots Organizations

1. We are grateful for these and other organizations that are committed to sustainability of land and people in the heartland.

2. Ed Chitwood, member of the American Raw Milk Producers Pricing Association (ARMPPA), as quoted by Patrick Slattery in "Students Learn New lessons Demonstrating for Farmers," *Times Review,* Diocese of LaCrosse, March 9, 2000.

3. Abbot Brendan Freeman, quoted by Tony Ends, *Janesville Gazette,* July 31, 1998. Conference cosponsored by CCLP and the Town and Country Association of the United Methodist Church: "Churches and Land Issues."

4. Examples of such organizations: Iowa Citizens for Community Improvement (ICCI) that supports people in organizing action around chosen people's chosen issues. Wisconsin Citizen Action (WCA) helped build a coalition around family farm protection that brought together farm, environment, conservation, consumer, and church groups.

5. Kinsman, as shared with the CCLP Ethics Committee.

6. Robert Karp, quoted by Mary Nevans-Pederson in "Rural Living Promoted," *Telegraph Herald* (Dubuque, IA), October 27, 2002. Speaking at the CCLP Rural Life Gathering "Passion for Rural Life."

7. In 1998, Sandra Simonson Thums and Miriam Brown, OP, received the annual Friends of Rural Ministry award from the Center for Theology and Land (CTL) of the University of Dubuque and Wartburg Seminaries. Sandra thought it significant that CTL honored lay and religious vocations and encouraged women to take leadership roles in church ministry.

8. Two examples: The Women, Food and Agriculture Network (WFAN) crosses several states with an interactive e-mail list-serve and produces a substantive newsletter; they are active regarding political issues. Wisconsin Women for Sustainable Farming Network (WWSFN) is supportive and practical for women in farming; they share personal experiences, technical information, and marketing strategies. They recently published among themselves "Women in Change: Tales and Teachings from Our Farms."

9. Audrey Arner, "Women in Agriculture: Gleaning a New Relationship with the Land and Each Other," *The Land Stewardship Letter,* December 2000, p. 2–4.

10. Gerard Manley Hopkins, "God's Grandeur," in *Poems of Gerard Manley Hopkins,* The First Edition with Preface and Notes by Robert Bridges. Edited with additional Poems, Notes, and a Biographical Introduction by W. H. Gardner. Third Edition, New York, Oxford University Press, 1948, p. 70.

11. Camy Matthay, participant from Wisconsin in the November 2003 three-day People's March to Miami protesting the proposed FTAA (Free Trade Area of the Americas). E-mail article, "The Enemy Is Profit," December 4, 2003.

12. Anne Kanten, quoted by Rev. Lowell Bolstad, *Family Farm or Factory Farm? Time to Choose,* Prairie Farm Press, 1982, p. 47.

13. Eva Jensen, "Table Agenda: Interconnectedness of the Issues," at "Come to the Table" conference sponsored by CCLP and ELCA Rural Office, June 21, 2000.

14. "'Top 10' Organizing Tips," Julianna Johnston, Iowa Citizen Action Network, 1993.

Chapter 7: Local Communities

1. Miriam Brown, OP, describing "The Role of Churches in the Community," a process developed by the CCLP Ethics Committee. See "Rural Spirituality Team," p. 170.

2. Margot Ford McMillen, "Tomato Days," *Yes,* Summer, 2000, pp. 40–43.

3. Adam Warthesen, "When Democracy Comes Home to Stay," *The Land Stewardship Letter,* October/November 2003, p. 5. (*www.landstewardshipproject.org).*

4. Miriam Brown, OP, "The Soul of Community Leadership," Fennimore, Wisconsin, April 26, 2000.

5. "Role of Churches in the Community" process.

6. Cornelia Butler Flora, "Innovations in Community Development," *Rural Development News,* September 1997, p. 3 (Phone: 515-294-8321). *www.ag.iastate.edu/centers/rdev/RuralDev.*

7. Kathleen Vinehout, organizer and emcee, Alma, Wisconsin.

8. Luther Snow, facilitator of area event, Alma, Wisconsin, author of *Organization of Hope: A Workbook for Rural Asset-Based Community Development,* published by ABCD Institute.

9. Tony and Catherine Jantsch, *Rural Roots,* of the former Rural Ministry Education Institute, March/April 1990, p. 3.

Chapter 8: Institutions

1. Dennis R. Keeney, "A Matter of Unfinished Business," *Leopold Letter,* Spring, 1999, p. 1.

2. Greg David, for this book, "Sustainability" discussions over a period of time in 2003.

3. Cornelia Butler Flora, "Extension and Place: Reducing Transaction Costs for Better Communities," *Rural Development News,* Vol. 24, No. 3, 2000, pp. 1–3.

4. Cornelia Butler Flora, "Market, State and Civil Society: Creating Advocacy Action Coalitions for Rural Development," *Rural Development News,* Vol. 24, No. 2, 2000, pp. 1–3.

5. John Ikerd, "The Industrialization of Agriculture: Why We Should Stop Promoting It," presented at the Harold F.

Breimeyer, 1995 Agricultural Policy Seminar, University of Missouri-Columbia, November 16–17, 1995 (*www.ssu.missouri.edu/faculty/jikerd).*

6. Richard Klemme, interview after "Value-Added" conference in Eau Claire, Wisconsin, February 2002.

7. Steve Stevenson, Center for Integrated Agricultural Systems, University of Wisconsin-Madison, "The Sacramental and Ethical Dimensions of Food Systems," CCLP Rural Life Gathering "Focus on Food," November 6, 1998.

8. Klemme, interview, February 2002.

9. "Bringing Healthy Food and Family Farmers into Madison Schools," article from the Research, Education, Action, and Policy Food Group (REAP), printed in *Family Farm Defenders,* Winter 2003, p. 18.

10. Tranel, Rural Spirituality Team, sharing for this book.

11. Frederick Kirschenmann, "An Open Letter to Iowa's Citizens," June 5, 2002 *(www.leopold.iastate.edu).*

12. Ambrose Koopmann, integrating essay, "Lay Ministry," April 1996.

13. Kirschenmann.

Chapter 9: Youth

1. James Frantzen, *James' Journal,* May 11, 2003. (*www.organicvalley.com/jamesjournal.php).*

2. Summarized from educational materials prepared by Brenda Ranum, Youth and 4-H Field Specialist, Iowa State University Extension, August 2000.

3. These responses come from a 2003 survey by Cathy Statz, Education Director for the Wisconsin Farmers Union (WFU). She involved young men and women ages 14–18 in a survey and discussion for this chapter. About half farm, others live in the country or small communities, a few in cities.

4. Bolstad, p. 5.

5. Rev. Cynthia Wolf, quoted by Jim Massey in "Pastors Gather to Discuss Issues of Rural Ministry," *Telegraph Herald* (Dubuque, IA), May 25, 1991.

6. Slattery, "Students Learn New Lessons."

7. Summarized from Peter L. Bensen, *All Kids Are Our Kids,* San Francisco, CA, 1997, as found in *Building Assets in*

Congregations, The Search Institute, 1998 *(www.search-institute.org).*

8. Robert Michael Franklin, cited by Leslie Scanlon, "Youth Ministry Professionals Work in a Rapidly Changing World," *The Presbyterian Outlook,* November 13, 2000, p. 4.

Chapter 10: Health Ministries

1. Barbara Pursey, written for this book. See "Rural Spirituality Team," p. 170.

2. Charlotte Halverson, quoted by Mary Nevans-Pederson in "Hark the Unheralded Church Workers," *Telegraph Herald,* April 17, 1999 *(halversc@mercyhealth.com).*

3. Roger Williams, notes from Power Point presentation at the Farm Crisis and Mental Health Conference, December 10–11, 1998, Omaha, Nebraska.

4. Joan Blundall, quoted by Peter G. Beeson, "Farm Crisis and Mental Health Summit: A Summary of Findings," *Party-Line,* newsletter of the National Association for Rural Mental Health, Winter, 1999, p. 31. This was a special issue on the summit held in Omaha, Nebraska, December 10–12, 1998.

5. Williams, Power Point presentation.

6. Roger Hannon, "How to Reach Farmers with Mental Health Services," *Party-Line,* p. 13.

7. Val Farmer, *Families and Rural Communities in an Era of Change,* published by the South Dakota Department of Human Services, Division of Mental Health through the National Institute of Mental Health, 1989, pp. 67–74.

8. Heffernan, "Mental Health and Ministry: The Vital Connection," *Party-Line,* p. 31.

9. Ibid.

10. Rev. Judith Dye, quoted by Beeson, *Party-Line,* p. 31.

11. Joan Blundall, "Mental Health Response to the Current Economic Crisis," *Party-Line,* p. 12. Also quoted by Beeson, *Party-Line,* p. 26.

12. Dr. Joanne Mermelstein, cited by Blundall, p. 12.

13. Rev. Norman White led many retreats in eastern Iowa during the 1980s. Phyllis Hughes, a retired attorney, donated legal services. For this and other civic contributions, Phyllis was entered into the Iowa Women's Hall of Fame.

14. Blundall, p. 32.

15. Mary Hayenger, "One Woman's Story: Choosing Life, Not Death," *Response,* journal of United Methodist Women, June 2000, p. 13.

16. Goodfellow, Rural Spirituality Team.

17. Rev. David Carlson, notes from class, "Interfacing Health Ministry/Health Care," Pastoral Care, Iowa Lutheran. Presently, Center for Spirituality and Healing, University of Minnesota.

18. Vickie Gratton, Director, Riverview Center, Galena, Illinois. (Phone: 1-888-707-8155).

19. Halverson, quoted by Nevans-Pederson in "Rural Life Promoted."

20. Quoted anonymously, "Parish Nurse Quotes," *Newsletter,* Kellogg Parish Nurse Project, Northwest Aging Association, January 30, 1992, p. 2.

21. Bonnie Kelly, "Parish Nursing: A Resource for Congregational and Community Health," *The Small Church Newsletter* of the Missouri School of Religion, September 1995.

22. Claudia Kalb, citing research of Lynda H. Powell, "Faith and Healing," *Newsweek,* November 10, 2003. p. 48.